Thomas G. Supensky   Davis Publications, Worcester, Massachusetts

CERAMIC ART IN THE SCHOOL PROGRAM

Acknowledgements

Gratitude is due my ceramic
students at The Maryland Institute
College of Art and at Eastern
High School, Baltimore, Maryland,
for their assistance with many
photographs. A special thanks
must go to George F. Horn for
his continuous encouragement,
and to Thomas Cole, poet and
fellow teacher, for reviewing the
manuscript.
                    Thomas G. Supensky

Consulting Editors:
Sarita R. Rainey
George F. Horn

Contents

TO JOHANNA

Introduction

Clay, that muddy, plastic stuff that pre-historic man pinched and squeezed together into three-dimensional form and subjected to heat until it became hard, has been passed down through the ages, collecting along the way the history of man, himself. The ceramic vessel indicates the progress of a civilization, its temperament, its moral code; it tells the story of an entire culture. And the ceramic vessel indicates the future of man. What is being done in clay today reflects the mood of our modern era.

The outward form of clay construction has certainly changed as well as the potter's thesis about what is good in ceramics; however, the basic techniques of forming clay, rolling out a coil or a slab, joining two pieces of clay, throwing on the potter's wheel, and general casting techniques have not changed. Once the techniques have been learned, expression, creativity, art can happen. Without a true expression of life, without a calculated guess or risk toward a new idea, the form will fail. There is no better medium than clay to explain the concept of form, to develop esthetic insight into design, texture, and growth of an object.

Ceramics should be a part of every art program. The expense of such a program is quite low, while ceramic equipment and materials are readily accessible in nearly all areas of the country. The introduction of clay into the art program decidedly supports the program's aims and goals no matter if at pre-school, elementary, or junior or senior high school levels. The field of ceramics is rapidly growing, becoming a major part of the fine arts program of many colleges, universities, and art institutions. True works of art in clay are found in homes, offices, stores, parks, and many other areas.

It is the purpose of this book to indicate the basic techniques of clay construction and to show a variety of good ceramic work in order to instill within the mind of the reader an open and free concept of ceramics so that he might be able to creatively express his feelings in clay.   *T.G.S.*

Foreword

The study of art can be a pleasurable and exciting experience. After a background understanding has been attained to help structure ideas, the world of self-realization is ever-widening. A difficult task, however, is to gain faith in one's own impressions rather than hold to what one thinks "should be" his impressions. Although it is comfortable and somewhat secure to re-do proven ideas, deeper personal value rests in becoming aware of all that is visually present in our daily lives to provide inspiration. The joy increases when this awareness leads on to independent, creative action.

This book offers important aids in background understanding; yet the text, photos, and ideas will be good for the reader only to the extent that he makes them good for himself. He can learn from the help presented, but he must envision and work beyond it. This means he must generate a creative drive. When such a drive is awakened in any person, no matter at what level of education or occupation in life, he tends to become an inventive, searching, and self-expressing creature. Motivation toward creative activity is based on the individual's struggle to express an idea.

A person who desires to become more creative starts by selecting and preparing for a specific need, followed by daily discoveries of growing needs. Such preparation is not a quick and easy matter. Time to develop sensitivity toward materials is a great help. Few have the courage and stamina to see the task through, completely. Repeated efforts to use the materials are necessary. *Unskilled manipulation of materials is frequently mistaken for spontaneity.* On the other hand, skillful work, too carefully composed, is unstimulating. Variations and unexpected relationships of parts should be considered as aids to creativity, to spontaneity, and to thinking beyond the ordinary.

One of the benefits coming from art is the opportunity to put ideas into some visible form, so they can be altered, strengthened, and compared to others' efforts. The least anyone can hope to accomplish is adding his fragment of understanding to the whole aspect of life. He can record his progress and whatever he achieves is so much for others to use or avoid. The product of one's efforts may be accepted or, perhaps more often, rejected by the artist or the public, or both. Rejection, however, should be taken, ideally, as a challenge to clarify meanings, simplify structures and be more direct in concept. History will continue to reconstruct from the discarded bits of our daily lives, accepted and rejected creative objects alike. Although our egos frequently make us unhappy and anxious for approval, for recognition, the deep enjoyment coming from any activity is generally in the work-stage itself.

Gaining a reliable working knowledge of construction materials, by repeated and near-constant usage, is one likely way to intensify creativity and to decrease the number of "failures." Failures and accidents should be anticipated when exploring an unfamiliar organization of forms. Repeated inability to accomplish set goals should be viewed as undesirable, however, because energy, time, and interest are dissipated. Whenever a project does not come up to expectation, self-doubt can be diluted by the realization that new knowledge has been attained and can be put to use in future undertakings.

One should go to his work of learning because it is important to him. The process of discovery is exhilarating.

Lyle N. Perkins, Ph.D.
Professor in Art (Ceramics)
University of Massachusetts

Since pre-historic times, clay, pliable, pleasing to handle, and having the quality to keep any shape given to it, has encouraged in man a sense of free, creative expression. Young and old alike derive a satisfaction from working with clay that seems to involve all the senses. Clay is a natural material for working directly with the hands. Squeeze it; pinch it and pull it apart. Push it together again and poke your fingers into it. Press it on a table top, hit it with your fist or open hand, and flatten it out. As a first experience, manipulating clay in this fashion gives you the "feeling" for such pleasant, inviting qualities that urge further exploration.

Clay can be found and used directly from nature. It is dug from deposits in river beds, creek and lake beds, fields, and hillsides. It is cheap and abundant, easy to prepare, and is often considered one of the best materials for three-dimensional art activities. Clay is also prepared commercially and may be purchased in wet or dry form. Many commercially prepared clays are a mixture of two or more different kinds of clays and have been purified by having non-clay materials removed, thereby insuring a smooth, consistent mixture.

Significantly, much that we know about man prior to recorded history has been discovered through his artifacts, many of which were fashioned in clay. It is true that necessity was a cause for early man's explorations with clay, but we must not overlook his human spirit, his mysterious imagination that soon developed to the point where he was creating for sheer aesthetic pleasure.

THE PHYSICAL QUALITIES OF CLAY: Even though there have been many remarkable discoveries and developments in new materials through scientific research, clay cannot truly be duplicated in the laboratory. Clay is composed, primarily, of many small grains or particles, the size and shape of which determine its plasticity, a quality that is extremely important to the potter. Plasticity is that property of clay to take and hold a shape that is given to it. Some clays are more plastic or workable than others.

Clay is the product of geologic weathering. It is formed in nature either right on the spot without being moved or by being transported by water, wind, or glacier. The process by which clay is produced is continual and takes a great many years. Chemically, clay is chiefly composed of silica and alumina. The average composition of the earth as a whole is nearly 60 percent silica and over 15 percent alumina. The earth also contains about 7 percent iron. When comparing a common red clay, it is found that the percentages of alumina, silica, and iron are nearly identical.

PRIMARY CLAY is that clay which has been formed on the site of its parent rock. Having a low degree of plasticity and being relatively free from impurities, primary clay is more difficult to locate and occurs

Stoneware pot of combined pinched and wheel-thrown forms by the author. The plastic qualities of the clay are readily visible in the throwing marks, the areas of joining, and the pinched-in area.

11

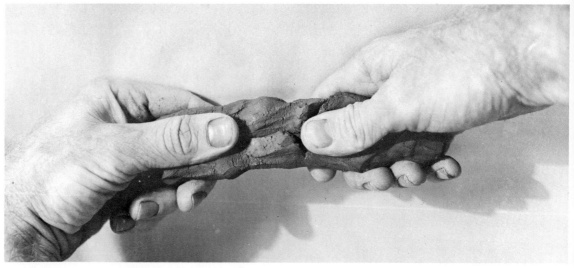

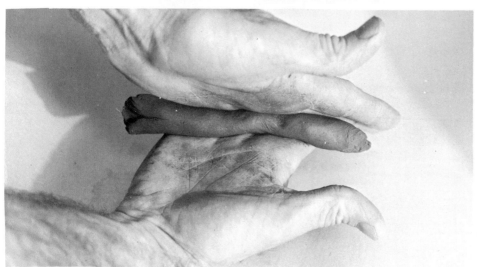

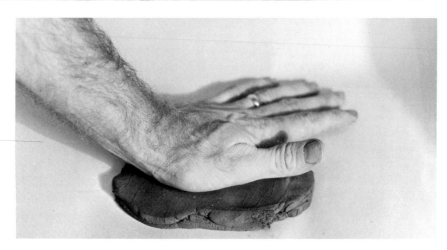

less frequently in nature than most other clays.

SECONDARY CLAY, the most common of clays, is developed as it is being carried from the site of the original rock formation by water, wind, or glacier. Water, the most prevalent transportation agent, washes the clay down streams and rivers and grinds it into small particles which settle in river or lake beds to form a mixture that is very plastic. During the long journey that the clay takes, it picks up certain impurities along the way, some of which add to the working ability of the clay. Carbonaceous matter is considered one of these impurities. Iron is also picked up along the way which gives the clay colors ranging from green to red-brown.

TYPES OF CLAY: *Earthenware*, a common material for making bricks, tiles, and similar products, is a very popular clay. Characteristic of earthenware clay is the fact that it fires at a low temperature and is usually red to red-brown in color. *Stoneware* clays are high-fire secondary clays, usually light in color, having qualities, particularly plasticity, that make them adaptable to almost any kind of clay construction. *Fire clays*, having the ability to withstand heat shock without cracking, deforming, or blowing up, are often added to stoneware or other clays to improve refractoriness and add to the textural quality. Fire clays give a certain amount of "tooth" to the clay body. *Ball clays*, very plastic secondary clays, are fairly free of iron and generally light buff in color. They contain considerable carbonaceous matter and form the bulk of throwing clay bodies. *Kaolins*, primary clays that are very coarse in particle size and comparatively nonplastic, are seldom used by themselves. Kaolins, being relatively free of impurities, are used in making pure white china or porcelain.

CLAY BODIES: Although many clays can be used without being altered, some must be changed so that they may best meet the needs of the potter. Such mixtures, prepared for a specific ceramic purpose, are referred to as clay bodies. While commercially prepared clay bodies are satisfactory for general purposes, it is often useful to know how to alter a clay to give it desired working properties.

Clay may be altered to

- change the degree of plasticity
- change the color
- change the texture
- change the shrinkage rate
- improve the fit of glazes
- change the maturing temperature.

To make clay more workable, add other clays or minerals having greater plasticity. A small amount of bentonite, a type of clay that is extremely plastic, is an excellent additive to improve plasticity. Ball clays improve plasticity.

Iron oxide is a common material used to

change the color of clays; however, other coloring oxides, such as cobalt, manganese, copper, rutile, nickel, chromium, cadmium, vanadium, or ilmenite can also be used.

To alter the texture of clay, to decrease the shrinkage rate and warping of clay, to strengthen it, and to make it more resistant to thermal shock, amounts of grog (fired clay that has been ground into more or less fine granules) may be added. Occasionally, other materials may be added in place of, or in addition to, grog to the clay such as sand, mica, or sawdust. Sawdust will burn out in the firing, of course.

To improve the fit of glazes and to change the maturing temperature, other materials must be added to make the clay more or less dense. By adding a material that lowers the melting point of the clay, it is possible to improve the fit of glazes and to change the maturing temperature.

Clay bodies, prepared essentially for throwing on the potter's wheel, are always very plastic, dense, and have a bit of roughness so that they will stand and not slump while still very wet. The height to which a potter is able to make a pot on the wheel is directly related to the workable qualities of the clay body.

On the other hand, clay to be used for modeling must be able to withstand thermal shock, must dry out quickly and shrink very little. Large amounts of grog (20 to 30 percent) added to clay will give it these necessary properties.

Casting clays are quite delicate and require prop-

erties that are often difficult to attain. Casting clay must be fine, smooth, easy to pour, and have a minimum of shrinkage. This fluid clay (clay slip) contains an ingredient called a deflocculant that causes the clay to be fluid without adding a great amount of water. A common deflocculant is sodium silicate. It causes the particles to disperse and become fluid. It should be noted that ordinary clay requires too much water to cast well, and it cracks and warps as it dries within the mold because of its greater shrinkage rate.

PREPARING CLAY: Clay may be obtained in dry powdered form or in semi-moist workable condition. Semi-moist clay is convenient and saves time in preparation; however, powdered clay is less expensive. In either case, clay should be ordered to meet predetermined needs.

When mixing powdered clay, pour water (normally equal in weight to the amount of clay) into a large non-porous container. Add the powdered clay and allow to stand for at least a day. Then mix with a wooden paddle or the hands until the clay is a smooth, creamy consistency. The less water used, the more difficult it is to mix. If the clay body to be mixed consists of two or more ingredients (for example, a stoneware clay, some fire clay, and some grog), then it is better to use enough water so that the clay body can be mixed with ease into a homogeneous consistency. Once the clay is mixed, it should be allowed to dry out a bit until it becomes semi-moist, stiff enough to knead into large balls, and then placed into an airtight container ready for use. The older the clay, the more plastic and work-

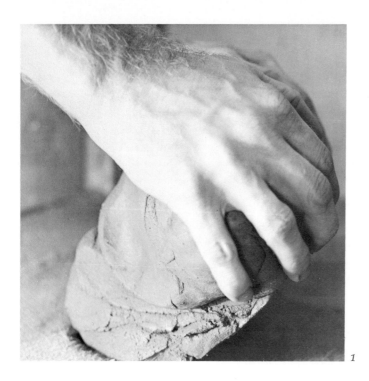

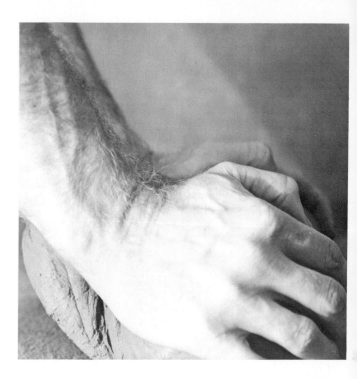
1

1. *A side view of the wedging process shows how the clay is folded into itself. Notice, the wrists are straight in preparation to press down on the clay.*

2. *At this point, the wrists are bent, indicating the twisting action of the hands.*

3. *A slight pressure to the side of the ball of clay keeps it from spreading out. The hands should aim for a central point while pressing downward.*

4. *A view of the wedging process shows the pattern made by the heel of the hands.*

5. *The wedged, or kneaded, piece of clay, is now ready for the process of clay construction.*

6. *Wedging clay with the feet is not a new method to the potter. The Chinese used this method in order to mix larger amounts of clay with less effort.*

4

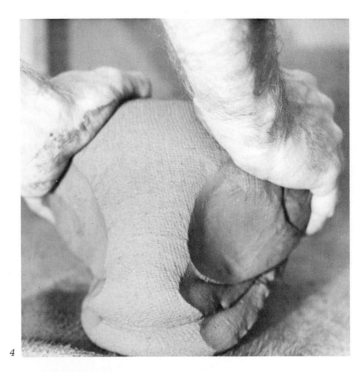

5

This group of bottles readily display the variety that can be achieved from a basic form, the sphere. Canadian potters listed clockwise: Bobbs, Ontario; Ross, British Columbia; Schwenk, British Columbia; Herman, Quebec; Levine, Saskatchewan; Davis, British Columbia; Dix, Quebec; Namer, Quebec; Bobbs, Ontario; Roy, Ontario.

able it is. It is interesting to note that the ancient Chinese used clay that was prepared by their grandparents and, in turn, they prepared clay for their grandchildren. For practical purposes, however, a couple of weeks of aging is all that is needed to accomplish the greatest improvement in clay. By adding some older clay to the new clay, the aging process is speeded up.

Clay ordered in semi-moist condition usually loses some of its moisture and should be cut into small pieces, a little water added, placed into an airtight container, and allowed to age for a few days.

WEDGING or KNEADING the clay is one of the most essential steps in the preparation of clay. In this way, the clay is developed into a uniform consistency, free of air bubbles.

Roll the clay by hand on a flat, porous surface (a plaster slab or a wooden table top) in the same way that a baker would knead dough. The lump of clay should be pushed down forcefully with the palms of the hands at about a forty-five degree angle to the wedging board. As the hands press down, a slight upward twist of the wrists will cause the clay to turn under slightly and mix more evenly. Turning the clay around after it has been wedged for a while and wedging it further, will ensure a completely uniform piece of clay. As the clay is turned under, with the twisting of the wrists, it can be slid forward slightly, thereby keeping the clay in the same spot on the wedging board. If the clay is unusually lumpy and inconsistent, cut the clay repeatedly on a stretched wire, recombining each time to disperse the lumps. Slamming the clay very hard on the flat surface is not necessary. The wedging process should be continued until it is felt that the clay is in the best possible condition for work. By checking the freshly cut surface of a piece of clay, it is easy to see if there are any remaining air bubbles and if there are any inconsistencies.

If a pug mill is available it may be used to eliminate the task of wedging. The pug mill works in much the same manner as a meat grinder, the clay being forced through a revolving screw. The more advanced models have a vacuum attachment that effectively refines the clay, removing all the air pockets and producing an extremely smooth, homogeneous clay mixture. However, even with the aid of a pug mill, it is advisable to wedge each individual piece of clay just prior to using it, because in time the outer surface of any clay may become inconsistent with the inner part.

STORING CLAY: Clay must be stored in an airtight container to keep it in its best workable condition. If the container is kept warm, damp, and dark, it contributes to the aging process. An old soft drink cooler makes an excellent storage space. Ceramic crocks and zinc-lined or galvanized iron containers are quite satisfactory. Bins may be made of wood or concrete and lined with a heavy duty plastic. Also, keeping a wet cloth over the clay helps to maintain a good humid atmosphere within the container.

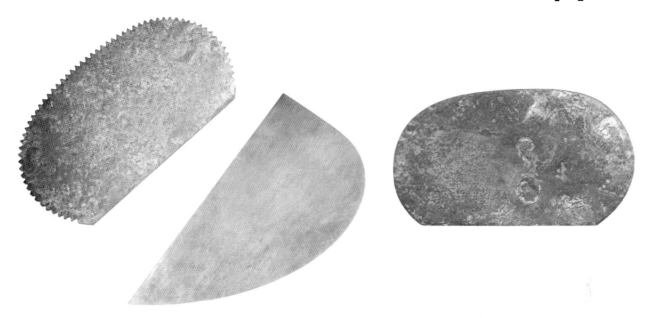

TOOLS

Man's first tools were his hands. Yet, he is intelligent enough to supplement his hands with other tools that enable him to produce things with greater precision and control. Tools are simply a continuation of the hands. In ceramics, the potter uses a great variety of tools. A tool is developed because there is a need for it, and the potter uses only those tools that he requires to complete his work. Many potters work with a minimum of a few simple tools while others find that they require many complex tools in their work. Each potter has different needs and uses those tools which best fit his needs. A typical list of tools required for work in ceramics includes such items as the following: (1) sponge, (2) knife, (3) pointed tool, (4) brush, (5) flexible metal rib, (6) modeling tool, (7) trimming tool, and (8) cutting wire.

A sponge can be utilized in many ways, just as most of the other tools that the potter uses. It is recommended that a large, natural sponge be used for general cleaning purposes and for large work such as applying a stain, engobe, or glaze to the surface of a pot. Sponges are also useful in applying textures to pots. A small, elephant-ear sponge is useful when working on the potter's wheel to sponge out excess water from the clay form. Sometimes a small piece of chamois is good to have because it acts as a sponge; but, as it soaks up excess water on the surface of the pot, it also smooths out the surface and can help produce an even and smooth lip.

A knife can be used to cut away excess clay, cut out shapes from rolled slabs of clay, carve surface decoration, cut holes in already made shapes, and to do many other jobs that arise. The knife need not be very sharp nor have a very pointed end.

A pointed tool, such as a hat pin stuck through a cork, is also useful for cutting and trimming. It may be used to scratch a design into the surface of a pot, make a small opening; or when working on the potter's wheel, it is used to trim the lip of the pot.

A brush is most useful in decorating pottery. A free-brush design (with clay slip, glaze, or stains) can quickly enhance the surface of a piece of ceramics. Brushes are also useful in applying slip to areas that are to be joined or in applying wax resists or liquid

opposite: "Sun Altar," a slab constructed,
28 inch high stoneware form with a dripped
glaze decoration. Maurice K. Grossman, U.S.A.

above: Three types of metal flexible ribs.
Wooden ribs are also useful and can be cut
and sanded into excellent tools.

bottom: An assortment of wire loop tools.
The loop may be sharpened in order to cut through the clay
more cleanly and with less pull.
center: The pointed tool serves many purposes. It must be
strong enough to do the job and long enough so that it is easy to handle.
top right: The pointed brush is used to make delicate designs,
free art work or patterns taken from the form of the brush itself,
while the flat brush is excellent for banding a pot
or for larger and bolder work.
1. Wooden clay modeling tools, usually associated with
sculpture, are quite useful when joining two pieces of
clay and getting at difficult to reach areas
that require smoothing and joining.
2. The cutting wire is useful in cutting through
leather-hard forms.

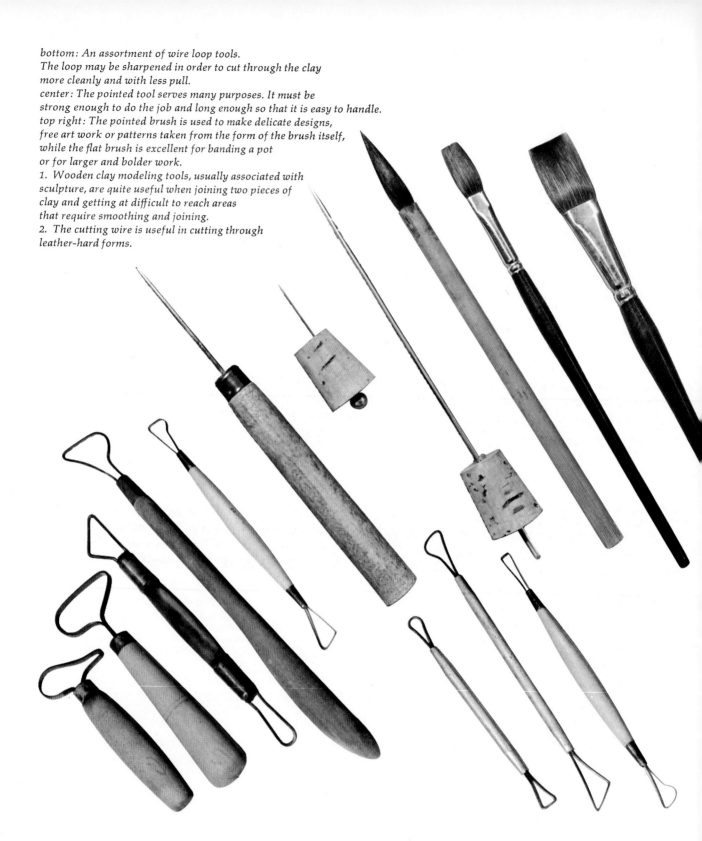

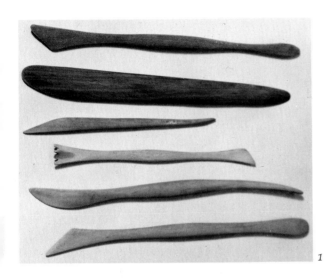

1

2

latex. A large Japanese brush is a good all-around tool.

A flexible metal rib, smooth-edged or with teeth, is excellent for shaping, scraping, modeling, leveling, carving, or texturing the surface of a piece of ceramics. Other types of ribs, such as rubber or wooden, can also be quite useful.

Modeling tools are helpful to join two pieces of clay, to get to places that are too awkward for the hand or fingers, to make a textured or decorative pattern, or to work on the potter's wheel, taking excess clay from the bottom of the thrown piece.

The trimming tool is also useful when working on the potter's wheel, and it can be used to help shape, decorate, or texture clay.

A cutting wire about 12 to 18 inches long with wooden dowels at each end for handles can be used to take a piece of thrown-ware from the wheel head as well as to cut through large hunks of clay. Trying to cut through a large piece of wedged clay with a knife is often difficult, and by simply passing a cutting wire through the clay the process is made quite simple. Nylon fishing line, about 30 pound weight, will also serve the purpose and eliminate the possibility of rusting.

Other tools that often have use in ceramics are a paddle for shaping, an apple corer for trimming, a small ear syringe for applying clay slips or glazes, and a ruler for measuring slab pieces and to act as a straight-edge when cutting clay slabs. Often some gadget, or "found" tool, is helpful, and potters seem to collect certain tools that work for their own individual purposes.

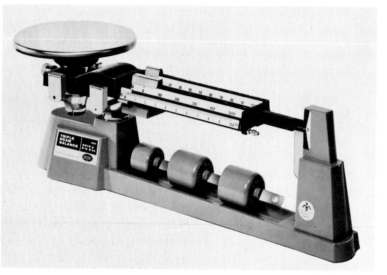

1

1. The triple beam balance is essential to glaze mixing; it may also be used to weigh out balls of clay to be thrown on the wheel when making a series of identical shapes. Ohaus Scale Corporation.

The potter's wheel takes many forms, and the potter chooses the form he likes best.

2. The kick wheel of today is greatly improved over the wheels of ancient civilizations with the introduction of lighter, stronger materials and a form-fitting "tractor" seat. Randall Pottery.

3. The treadle wheel allows the potter to stand while working. American Art Clay Co., Inc.

4. A top-loading electric kiln. American Art Clay Co., Inc.

5. A front loading, electric kiln. L and L Manufacturing Company.

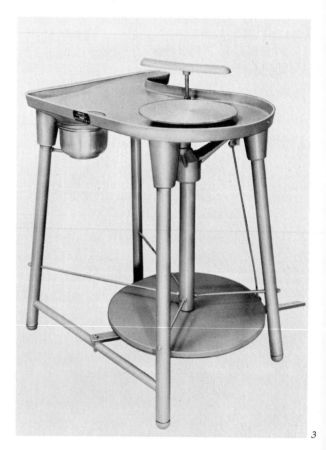

3

EQUIPMENT

It is difficult to tell where tools leave off and equipment begins. However, the potter has many forms of equipment at his disposal which aid his purpose. The only indispensable piece of equipment to the ceramist is the kiln. Other equipment may facilitate the ceramic process, but is often afforded only when practical. The potter's wheel is a common piece of equipment that offers its own dimension to ceramics. Other pieces of equipment that are nice to have, if practicable, are such things as a clay-mixing machine, a pug mill, a filter press, a damp room, a drying room, a ball mill, and balance scales. A clay-mixing machine, a pug mill, and a filter press all do essentially the same thing, which is mix clay. The traditional method of mixing clay by hand or even with the feet (as crushing grapes) may be a bit more tiring and time-consuming, but certainly less expensive. Sheets of plastic over semi-moist ceramics will serve the same purpose as a damp room; while a fan, a radiator, or hot sunshine are excellent subsitutes for a drying room. If commercially prepared glazes are utilized, a ball mill or balance scales would not be required. Other items such as wedging boards, working tables, sinks, shelves, rolling pins, burlap (or some such material), wire mesh screens, mortar and pestle, pyrometers, pyrometric cones, grog, sand, grinding wheels, cans, and bowls all have their uses and can be utilized as required.

When purchasing equipment for ceramics, it is important to purchase items that will last and that will do the job required. Often the kiln is too small, the potter's wheel is not powerful enough, or the clay mixer will not produce quickly enough. Small kilns are good for tests, but seldom serve the potter who wishes to make larger pieces. A solid kick wheel with good momentum has less chance of malfunction than a mediocre electric wheel. Electric wheels should be solidly constructed, with variable speeds, plenty of horsepower and turning strength, and nearly vibrationless.

Well cared for equipment will serve longest and best. Cleaning the equipment after every use will not only maintain it but provide a much better working environment.

4

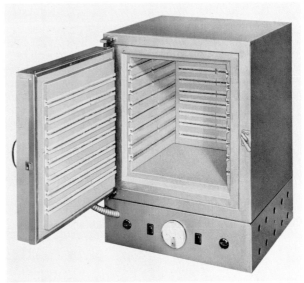

5

1. *Detail of pyrometer which measures the atmosphere within the kiln. L and L Manufacturing Company.*
2. *A motor powered clay mixer is one form of saving time for the potter. Randall Pottery.*
3. *The pug mill takes the place of many man-hours of work in preparing the clay. Dry powdered clay, or scrap clay, is placed into the hopper opening and water is added. The clay is forced by the screw action of the blades out the discharge tube, mixed and ready for the potter's hand. Walker Jamar Company, Inc.*
4. *With the development of strong, nearly vibrationless motors, the potter's wheel takes on a new look. This variable speed, electric potter's wheel saves much of the physical energy of the potter and allows him greater productivity. Skutt and Sons.*

1

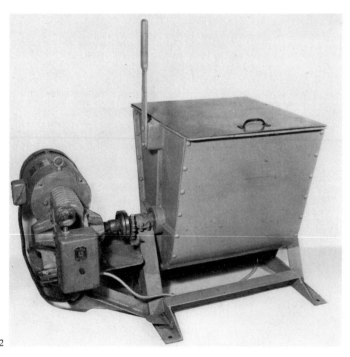

2

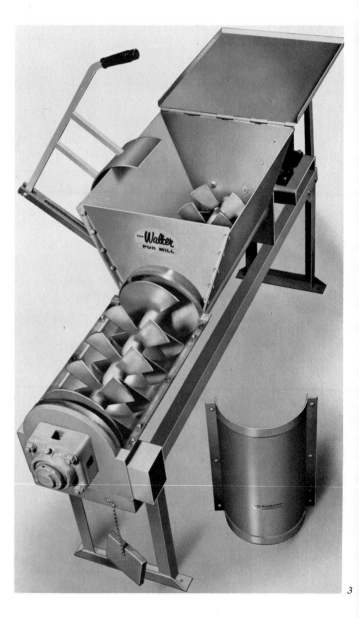

3

5. Two types of wheel heads for the potter's wheel. The rimmed head is made to hold a plaster bat that may be removed with the thrown piece still on it, while the flat head is usually used directly. Randall Pottery.

6. Molds used to make plaster bats on which to throw. Plaster bats are not only essential in throwing but may be used to help dry out very wet clay. Randall Pottery.

7. The banding wheel is a tool that gives the potter a better perspective of the form which he is constructing as he rotates it. Coil pots and other forms that are basically round are controlled better when constructed on a banding wheel.

5

6

7

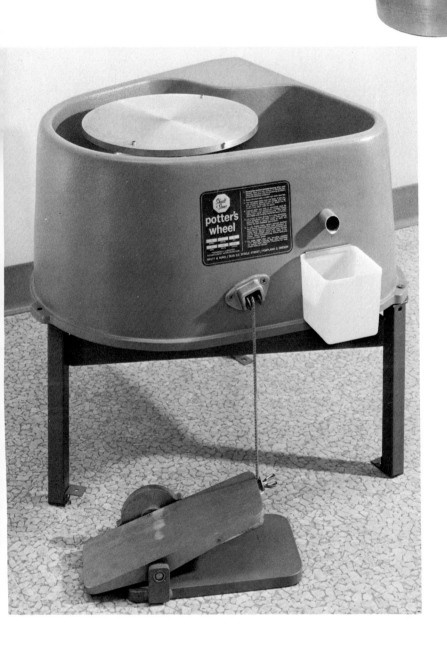

Sculptured slabs of a boy, cat, and quails.
Marguerite Wildenhain, U.S.A.

PART III: Clay Construction

The process of making something out of clay can be extremely simple as well as very complicated. It helps to know something about the specific clay body on hand, its degree of plasticity, its strengths or weaknesses. Even though clay can take any shape given to it, because of stress, improper balance of weight, incorrect methods of joining, or improperly constructed walls, it may not always hold. Some common categories of clay construction are as follows: (1) pinch, (2) coil, (3) slab, (4) mold and casting, (5) wheel thrown, and (6) combinations of other methods.

Pinch pots are the simplest forms to construct. A small ball of clay about the size of a tennis ball or smaller is pinched between the fingers and slowly revolved until there is an opening developed and finally until a small, usually round, bowl shape is formed with equally thick walls of about ¼ inch. Doing a pinch pot is a practical exercise in the beginning as it allows familiarity with the clay, its properties and limitations. It is possible to create some very unique forms in ceramics using the pinch method of construction.

Making a *coil pot* or coil structure is a favorite method of construction that stresses the importance of rolling out coils of clay and joining two pieces of clay together. The process is repetitious and slow, but the end product can be extremely pleasing and original. Normally, a small slab of clay is rolled out to form the base or foot of the structure. The first coil, as well as each succeeding coil, must be attached to the other so as not to come apart in drying or firing. The method for joining two pieces of clay can vary; however, the idea is to weld the two pieces together as though they were one. Usually, both surfaces are cross-hatched with a pointed tool, a rib with saw-toothed edges or even a fork. Then clay slip is brushed onto both surfaces to be joined, after which the two pieces are pushed together. If the shape is intended to flare out, the coils should be made longer with each layer and just the opposite if the shape is intended to come inward. As each coil is added, it is advisable to smooth together or wedge together the interior of the top coil with the one directly underneath it. The reason for this is that if the shape closes in and the opening at the top is smaller than the potter's hand, it will not be possible to smooth out the inside surface. A rough interior surface is difficult to clean or wash, while the outside surface can be left alone to show the coil pattern or can be textured to create added interest to the shape.

One type of clay construction that is actually an extension of working with coils is the *slab method.* Instead of joining many coils of clay to make a shape, slabs of clay are rolled out with a rolling pin to form entire walls or sides or even the entire structure. The slab method is very quick and offers many possibilities. A ball of clay is paddled a bit flat and placed between two long, ¼-inch thick sticks on a surface such as burlap (newspaper works fine). The sticks act as guides when the rolling pin is rolled over the clay so that the clay will be uniform in thickness. The rolling pin (or whatever cylinder-shaped object is used) should be porous so that the clay will not stick to it. If the clay is too soft, it should be allowed to stiffen up a bit more to prevent it from sticking to the rolling pin. Do not let the clay accumulate on the surface of the rolling pin. If paper is used under the clay and should it stick to the clay, there should be no concern because it will burn off during the firing. It is important, as in all forms of clay construction, to have patience with the clay; and if it is too soft and wobbles and droops while it is being put together, it is best to let the clay dry a bit. Each slab is joined just as in the coil method; and sometimes overlapping the two slabs or adding a small coil of clay to the joint will give enough extra clay to pinch or work around, and thus more strongly join the slabs. In order to prevent warping or cracking, it is best to join clay that is of the same consistency.

1

3

1. *Centering*
2. *Opening*
3. *Raising*
4. *Forming*

30

2

4

Once the main body of the slab structure is put together, it can be paddled, shaped, cut into, twisted, or otherwise formed into the final concept. Other appendages, handles, spouts, decorative clay forms, wads of clay, coils, decorations and textures can also be added if desired. The slab is often combined with coils or thrown shapes.

There are many methods of clay construction that involve the use of a *mold*. A simple type of mold that lends itself to the slab technique is the drape mold where a slab of clay is simply draped into or onto a form and allowed to stiffen enough to hold its own shape. It is better to drape clay into a shape rather than onto one. Because clay will shrink as it dries, if it is placed over a rigid form such as a rock, plaster hump, or other such form, it will develop cracks and split apart. However, if the slab is draped into a form such as a plaster impression or a piece of cloth draped into a wastecan, there is nothing to stop it as it shrinks, and success is more easily obtained. For decorative purposes, clay is often pressed into molds of plaster, wood, or other material. There are many other types of molds, such as casting molds, most of which are used in the commercial field of ceramics. While casting is an interesting technique, it can be complicated; and often the true artistic concepts that can be derived from working with clay are overshadowed by the process.

Another technical process of clay construction is working on the *potter's wheel*. However, the potter's wheel, once the technique is learned, offers a whole world of creative experiences. To the casual observer, throwing on the wheel seems simple, quick, and fun, almost as if something magic were taking place as the clay spins around within the potter's hands. The potter's wheel is always a big attraction. Nevertheless, there are few persons able to create something at their first attempt. Here patience is very important, as the novice will soon discover, if he wishes to be successful at the wheel. The process can be broken down into four basic steps: centering, opening, lifting or raising, and forming.

*"Moon Form," an 18 inch high slab and wheel
pot with added clay, carved and stamped.
Maurice K. Grossman, U.S.A.*

The basic tools for working on the potter's wheel are the hands. As occasion calls, however, certain other tools are utilized. Once the technique of wheel throwing is learned, the world of ceramic creativity is greatly expanded so that wheel-thrown shapes can be easily combined with slab, coil and/or pinched shapes. Thus is developed the *combination* pot. Many slab pots have wheel-thrown feet, lips, handles, etc. Simply by cutting into leather-hard thrown pieces, cutting them in half or in sections, new arrangements and new shapes can be created. The method of joining clay remains the same. If slab and thrown pieces are joined together, they should both be of the same consistency so that they dry evenly and do not come apart at the seams.

In the case of many functional items, such things as handles must be added to the body of the ceramic piece. Handles should be functional and fit the shape of the pot on which they are to be joined. Simple handles could be a small thrown cylinder, a thrown cylinder that has been cut in half, a coil of clay, or a knob of clay. One type of handle that is quite effective and illustrates the real plastic quality of clay is the *pulled handle*. Pulling a handle is a technique that takes some practice.

Once any piece of ceramics is made, care must be taken in the *drying process.* If clay is allowed to dry too quickly, it may crack or split and warp; therefore, it must be allowed to dry slowly. Usually the finished piece should be covered well for a day and for a period of about one hour a day until the clay gets leather-hard. Then the clay can be dried in the open air. Clay must be dried completely before it is fired. A simple test is to put the clay next to a window pane; and if the slightest bit of condensation is noticed to collect on the glass, the clay is not dry enough. Those pieces that are ready for firing might be placed in a hot, dry area before firing, such as near a kiln that is being fired or next to a radiator.

When clay is ready to work with, it is commonly called semi-moist clay. However, once the shape has been made and slowly begins to dry, it is no longer soft and pliable. It will crack when bent. At this stage it is called leather-hard clay. Leather-hard clay can be carved and slightly modeled or finished, and it can even be polished with a hard, smooth tool. Once a clay shape has been dried completely, it is called bone-dry ware. Semi-moist ware, leather-hard ware, and bone-dry ware are all greenware; not until greenware has been fired does it change chemically so that it no longer can be wetted and made back into soft, workable clay. Any piece of greenware that is not to be fired, or any scrap greenware can be placed in a large container, water added, and then worked into good semi-moist clay again. Never throw scrap clay away unless it has become contaminated by some foreign matter, such as plaster, etc. A can for scrap clay is a handy item to have around.

During the construction of a piece of ceramics, when it becomes leather hard or bone dry, if a piece is broken, chipped, or if a crack develops, it is normally best to begin all over again rather than to try to put the object together again with slip. However, if the broken area seems simple and mending it must be tried, instead of using water, use vinegar to make some clay slip, add a little fine grog or sand to the slip, and then burnish the mended area with a hard tool such as the back of a spoon. This process should be repeated if the crack reappears; and if the potter has luck, the crack or break can be mended.

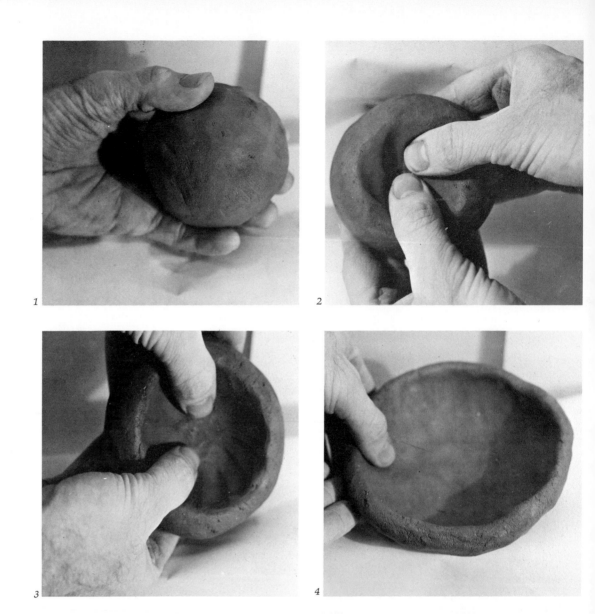

1

2

3

4

9

34

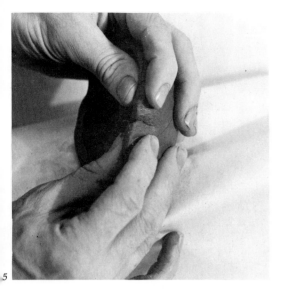

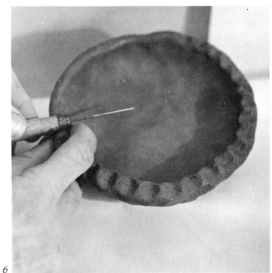

5

6

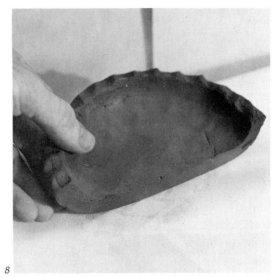

7

8

10

11

1. The ball of clay only waits the potter's trained fingers to press it into whatever form he desires.

2. The first stage of making a pinch pot. The thumbs and fingers press the clay into a gradual depression with even wall thickness.

3. The opening gets larger as the hand rotates the clay and thins out the clay.

4. The lip of the form must be kept clean and even.

5. If a crack develops in the clay, it must be mended by pushing the clay together. Adding excessive amounts of water to smooth over cracks and other blemishes is not necessary and usually causes slumping and a general control problem.

6. The lip of the pinch pot, as with any pot, may be decorated as desired. Thin lips, or lips with sharp edges, are not practical and should be avoided.

7. Working over the surface of clay with a metal flexible rib gives the form a definite line and clearly indicates the maker had control over the clay rather than the clay taking whatever form gravity would allow.

8. The wall thickness of any form should be even.

9. A pinched porcelain pot with two incised lines and a clear porcelain glaze. Ruth Duckworth, U.S.A.

10. Pinched and slab constructed porcelain pot, 6 inches high, with a small amount of copper wash and a semi-mat glaze. The free creative forms pinched on top offer an interesting contrast to the base which lifts the entire form into life. Ruth Duckworth, U.S.A.

11. The pinch pot can take many forms; a quick, spontaneous manipulation often produces the most satisfactory form.

1

2

3

4

5

8

6

9

7

1. A coil constructed garden sculpture, six feet high. The method of coil construction is one of the best ways to build such a large piece. Nino Caruso, Italy.

2. The base of the coil pot is normally made from a slab of clay.

3. Cross-hatching the base. Coils are rolled out and placed one on top of the other. Cross-hatch each coil and add a bit of clay slip to ensure proper joining of each one.

4. Attaching the first coil to the base is easily accomplished with a modeling tool.

5. Cross-hatching each coil and applying clay slip ensures complete joining.

6. A saw-toothed metal flexible rib is an excellent tool for cross-hatching.

7. The interior of the coil pot is joined solidly while the outside awaits the creative hand to apply a texture.

8. Smoothing the interior of the pot allows for easy cleaning and if the form is open, such as a bowl or plate, the smoothed surface lends itself to brush decoration as well.

9. This unique, foot-long, coil construction reflects a sense of balance that is important in ceramic construction. Nino Caruso, Italy.

37

1

1. "Owl Form," pinched coil decoration, 24 inches high, This stoneware shape demonstrates a simple, bold form with equally strong texture. Maurice K. Grossman, U.S.A.

2. The textural variations that can be achieved by the coil method of clay construction often give a hint to the procedure.

3. Clay can be manipulated to give soft, subtle qualities as seen in this ceramic leopard. Paul Bogatay, U.S.A.

4. The suggestion of the human form, as seen in this four foot coil vase, relates strongly to the method of construction. Nino Caruso, Italy.

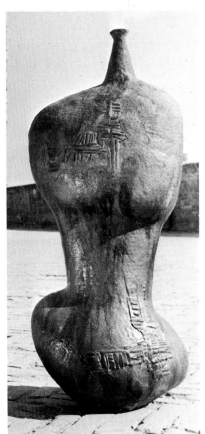

4

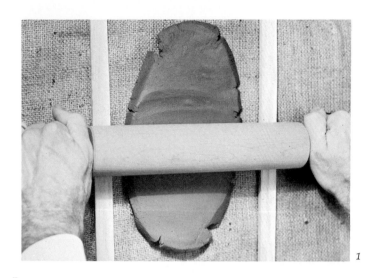

40

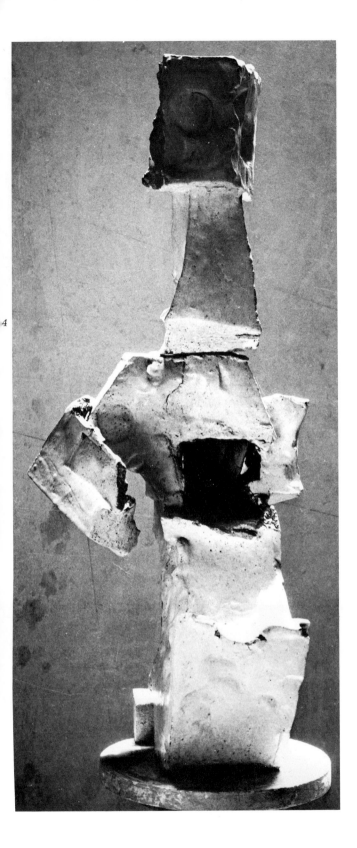

4

5

1. Rolling out a slab of clay with a rolling pin.
2. Detail of the relief sculpture shows painter-like approach to texture and form in clay.
3. A six-foot relief sculpture fired to cone 10 utilizes the slab method of construction. Ken McElroy, U.S.A.
4. The slab construction suggests rectangular form as seen in this stoneware sculpture. Guido Gambone, Italy.
5. The textural tone of the slab pot, just as with the coil pot, has its own unique qualities. The quickly shaped slab form is expertly displayed as three goblets. Patrick Kennedy, U.S.A.

1

1. "Interrupted Diagonal," a slab constructed stoneware form that excites the
sense of direction and balance. John
Stephenson, U.S.A.
2. The basic slab constructed box can be
cut open and rearranged in unlimited
creative ways. A wheel-thrown shape, cut
in half, has been added to this slab form.
3. Paper may be stuffed into the slab form
in order to prevent the top from slumping
until it gets dry enough to hold its shape.
The paper, naturally, burns out during the
firing.
4. All the parts of a slab constructed pot
should be measured and cut prior to putting
them together.
5. Even though there are less areas to join
in the slab pot than in the coil pot, the
technique is the same and equally important.
6. Applying clay slip to the cross-hatched
area acts somewhat as a glue when joining
two pieces of clay.
7. The cut slabs of clay should be joined
only when they are stiff enough to stand
without slumping. Patience is important
when working with larger forms so that
the slabs will hold their shape.
8. A small coil of clay wedged into the joint
of two slabs aids in stronger joining.
9. The slab construction gains added
strength as more sides are connected.
10. The slab is nothing but an extension
of the coil and this bird-like form has been
constructed by thin slabs of clay, almost in
coil form. Dora Pezic-Mijatovic, Yugoslavia.

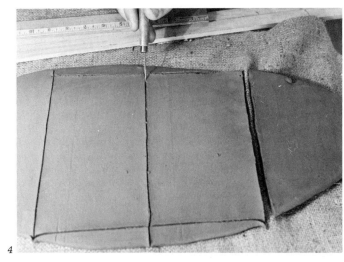

4

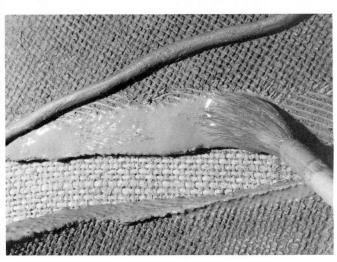

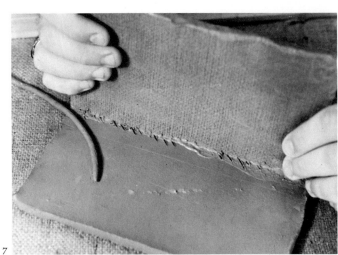

7

10

43

1. The bottle and pitcher take a fresh look with flat slab sides. Guido Gambone, Italy.

2. This slab-built, very groggy pot retains a powerful form with a warm textural quality. Ruth Duckworth, U.S.A.

3. The techniques used to produce this 16-inch slab constructed stoneware form involve more than a simple process. The newspaper mat impressions are obtained by pressing the clay into a newspaper matrix after it has been coated with a white clay slip. After the bisque firing, the form is rubbed with a black stain, thus producing the newspaper effect. John Stephenson, U.S.A.

4. The careful craftsmanship can readily be seen in this stoneware lantern, yet the feeling of spontaneity is present with the subtle twist of the design on the top. Paul Bogatay, U.S.A.

5. The slab may be draped around a cylindrical form. This form presents an interesting texture. Ljerka Jovan Saric, Yugoslavia.

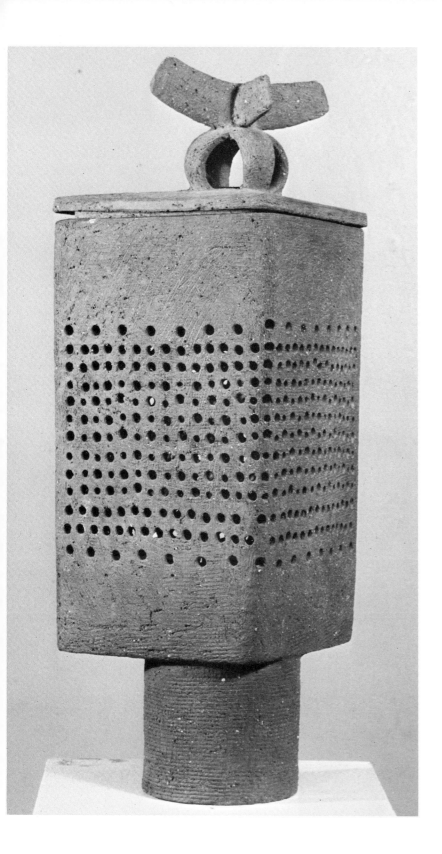

5

1. The precision of the geometric form is handsomely presented by the method of slip casting. Nino Caruso, Italy.

2. The advantage of the cast form is to duplicate a great number of identical forms. However, it is important when designing a dinner set that the forms be related in basic shape as seen in the handsome series, "Opi," designed by Arch. Franco Bettonica and produced by Gabbianelli, Italy.

3. Prize winning ceramic lamp designed by Marcello Cuneo and produced by Gabbianelli, Italy.

4. Reproducing identical forms in clay is best done by the casting method. Nino Caruso, Italy.

5. The concept of drawing the viewer's eye around the form has been excellently executed by the applied design of Roberto Arioli, produced by Gabbianelli, Italy.

6. A slightly squared bowl of a coarse clay body by Eva Staehr-Nielsen, produced by Saxbo Stentoj, Denmark.

4

6

5

47

1. *A practical feature of any dinnerware series is that the forms can be stored easily. The ability to stack one form into the other for saving space is artistically done as seen in parts of the dinner service, "Blue Line," designed by Grethe Meyer for Den Kongelige Porcelainsfabrik A/S, Denmark.*

2

2. Often the most difficult form to create is
the simple one. Other parts of the dinner
service, "Blue Line."

1. Trimming tools, a pointed tool, a flexible metal rib, and a small elephant-ear sponge are plenty for normal work. An old rubber heel is good to clean excess clay from the plaster wheelhead so as not to chip plaster into the clay. A pair of calipers is useful as a measuring device when making such forms as lids. A small container of water is necessary, also.

2. A well wedged ball of clay about the size of a grapefruit is placed on the wheel head as close to the center as possible.

3. The wheel head is moistened a bit and the ball of clay slightly slammed to the plaster bat to ensure that the clay is stuck and will not slip off during the throwing process.

4. Wet both hands with water and place them around the ball of clay. The wheel head is turned at a very fast rate in a counter-clockwise direction. The idea is to get the clay exactly in the center of the wheel head with no wobbles or bumps. There is no one correct way to work on the potter's wheel but there are certain concepts that all good potters follow. The centering process should be thought of as applying a direct, wilfull force to the clay ball; be the master of the clay, do not let the clay master you; get comfortable; release the clay gradually rather than with a jerk. Jerking away from the clay at any point will throw it off balance again. Both arms should be supported against the body and whenever possible both hands should be touching at some point. A steady control of breathing usually helps in centering the clay.

5. The steady pressure that is applied to the clay is best directed from the body to the clay with the base of the left hand while, at the same time, pulling inward with the finger tips of the right hand.

6. The centered piece of clay should be formed into a semi-beehive shape with a slight undercut at the base.

3

6

7. *This thrown stoneware bottle, 8 inches high, was indented when the form was quite soft and scratched with a wood tool. The semi-mat glaze picks up the throwing and making marks of the pot. Dorothy W. Perkins, U.S.A.*

7

1

5

6

1. Next begins the second phase in wheel throwing: making the opening. Again, there is no set way to make the opening except that it should be done directly. A suggested method is to use the right thumb, curved outward, with the right hand touching the left hand so that both hands are working in unison.

2. The thumb is thrust steadily, but with directness, straight down into the clay until the base thickness is about ⅜ of an inch.

3., 4. At this point the thumb can be pulled inward at the first joint so as to make a slight ridge on the inside of the opening at the base.

5. It is important to keep the thumb curved outward so that as it is forced into the clay, an air pocket is developed between the thumb and clay wall which prevents the clay from sticking to the thumb and throwing the opening off center.

6. Following the opening of the clay, the next procedure is to raise or lift the clay upward. The hand that during the opening procedure was inside the clay, the right hand, is now on the outside of the centered clay while the left hand moves from the outside to the inside.

9

3

4

7

8

10

7., 8. Both hands should be touching and, depending upon the size of the ball of clay, at least two fingers should be placed inside the opening.

9. The thrown form is first circular. However, it may be paddled, pulled, twisted, or otherwise formed into any shape. Vase and bowl in stoneware. Niels Refsgaard, Denmark.

10. An exaggerated lip gives a unique feeling in these two forms. Finn Lynggaard, Denmark.

1., 2. The grooves that were made on the outside with the right fingers and on the inside with the right thumb, while opening the ball, are now grasped by the outside right fingers and the inside left fingers. As the wheel is constantly turning, the "ring" of clay that the fingers are holding is slowly and steadily brought upward with a constant, direct pressure that is strongest at the bottom and that slowly releases as it reaches the top or the lip of the pot.

3., 4., 5. The raising process is repeated a number of times until the pot has an even wall thickness of about ¼ to ⅜ of an inch. The lip of the pot should be kept clean and neat and just slightly thicker than the rest of the wall. If excess water accumulates inside the pot it is advisable to sponge out the water rather than leave it inside where it will cause the clay to soften, possibly slump, and perhaps cause cracking in the base during the drying process.

6. Between each raising, the lip of the pot should be brought inward by pressing the upper wall of the pot together with both hands on the outside. This is done to prevent the lip from getting too wide and out of control. (The wider the shape, the slower the wheel should be turned, as centrifugal force will tend to pull the clay wider and wider if caution is not taken.)

7., 8. As the piece of clay gets taller and taller, it is not possible to have both hands touching; however, they must work as one.

9. Joining two thrown shapes not only is a method of obtaining greater height but, as in this form, offers the opportunity to create a contrasting texture and line, by the author.

1

2

5

6

54

3

4

7

8

9

1., 2. If the clay was not well centered, if the opening was not properly centered, or, if during the raising of the pot the clay was thrown a bit off center, the lip of the pot will surely be uneven and not level. When this happens the uneven area should be removed by trimming with a pointed tool. The left hand is used to hold the pot at the lip and the right hand holds the pointed tool, touching the left hand at some convenient place. The point is passed through the clay as it revolves and just at the moment when the ring of clay is cut through, the left hand lifts off the excess clay, leaving a level lip once again.

3. The lip can be thickened or adjusted by the fingertips of both hands.

4. The lip should indicate a stopping point for the pot, whether it be subtle or exaggerated. Three thrown stoneware pots, by the author.

5., 6. The finished pot, or cylindrical shape, should have an even wall thickness and enough base so that the pot can be trimmed later when it is leatherhard. Usually there is a slight excess of clay remaining at the base of the pot and it can be trimmed away with a trimming or modeling tool. The final step is to shape the pot into an individual artistic creation and, within limits, this is easily done. Before deciding on the amount of clay to be thrown, it is wise to plan what the end shape will be. When centering, opening, and raising the clay, adjustments

can be made so that the desired shape will result. There are specific skills related to different shapes such as bowls, plates, and bottles; however, the overall throwing concept is the same.

3

4

6

7

7. A genuine quality of plasticity is obvious
in this stoneware, covered jar. The forms are
directly related to the pliant characteristic
of the rolled lip and the freely pinched sides.
Susanne Stephenson, U.S.A.

1

3

4

2

5

6

1. Stoneware jar with blue glaze by Conny Walther, Denmark.
2. The necked-in area of a pot may extend into a long spout or simply become a small, but highly important, part of the form. Patrick Kennedy, U.S.A.
3., 4. Necking-in the cylinder. The process of making a bottle begins with throwing the basic cylinder form and then forming the lower part to the desired shape. The neck of the bottle is pulled inward by a steady grip of the fingers around the cylinder, beginning gradually and slightly below the point at which the shape is to curve inward. Only the fingers should touch the surface of the cylinder, not the entire hand; the less surface tension, the less likely the spout will twist or tear.
5. As the neck is brought inward, it tends to thicken, and should be raised from time to time in order to maintain equal wall thickness throughout the form.
6. The bulging body of this 6 inch stoneware lidded bowl is accentuated by the added base. Dorothy W. Perkins, U.S.A.

1. From the basic thrown shape is developed a more complicated, yet personal, interpretation by combining thrown pieces, by the author.

2. The repeated form of the pattern relates strongly to the overall form of covered jar on the left, just as the banded lines work with the line created by the lidded pot on the right. Gertrud Vasegaard, Denmark.

3. A successful combination of the slab and wheel methods of construction relates a positive contrast of the well-defined thrown areas to the free, rough-textured slab section. Maurice K. Grossman, U.S.A.

4. Bringing in the neck area magnifies any slight uneven wall thickness that may have developed in centering, opening, or raising. This uneven quality will appear at the top of the lip and should be cut off with a pointed tool.

5. The lip can take many forms; however, by experimenting, a variety of successful answers can be obtained that will give the lip a feeling of importance, signifying a point of conclusion on the form that has equal artistic strength with the entire pot.

6. Paddling the symmetrical thrown shape into a new and exciting expression, and adding a carved, low relief and multi-colored glaze, changes an otherwise uninteresting form into an exciting and lively pot. Raul Angulo Coronel, U.S.A.

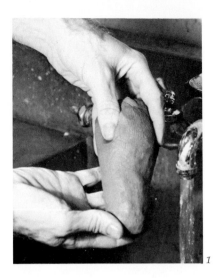

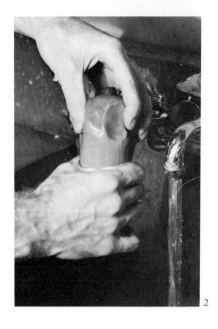

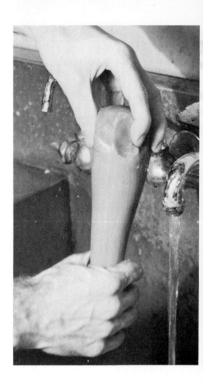

1. A ball of clay is wedged and rolled into a somewhat large cylinder-like shape.

2. The clay is grasped firmly at the top, letting the cylinder hang. The other hand, always moist with water, grasps the clay directly underneath the first hand and gently pulls downward, allowing the clay to pass or slip through the hand at even pressure.

3., 4. Working near a running tap gives the constant water supply that is needed to lubricate the clay. Pulling the hand beyond the clay in a follow-through fashion will prevent accumulation of excess clay at the end of the handle, thus resulting in an evenly tapered handle.

5., 6. The weight of the clay and the gentle pulling process will cause the clay to stretch into a long, tapered shape.

7. As soon as the clay appears to be the right thickness for the handle desired, the clay is turned upright, allowing the clay to make a natural handle-like curve or bend. The clay will be very soft, after soaking up lots of water, and should be allowed to stand until it gets a bit stiffer. After an hour or so, when the shape is able to hold its own, the excess clay is cut off one or both ends, and the handle applied to the pot.

8. The exciting thing about pulled handles is not only their graceful, plastic quality, but the method in which they are applied to the pot. Of course, both surfaces should be cross-hatched and slip applied; however, underneath the upper part of the handle and at the base of the hand,

a very free pressing together with the finger creates a handsome "making" mark as well as more completely joining the handle to the pot.

9. The simple addition of handles creates a new concept to the thrown form. Patrick Kennedy, U.S.A.

4

5

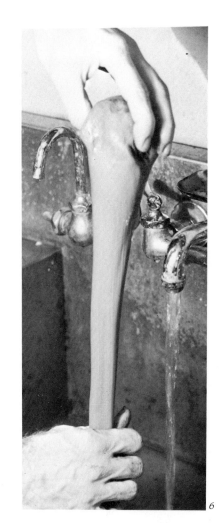

6

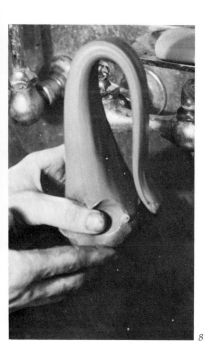

8

9

1. *The added clay bosses give this 26 inch stoneware vase not only an interesting texture, but added weight in the shoulder area thereby "lifting" the pot to life. Lyle N. Perkins, U.S.A.*

2. *Combining other materials with clay is a possibility that often leads to satisfying results as seen in this ceramic sculpture. Conny Walther, Denmark. Den Permanente Collection.*

3. *The strength of the thrown form allows for larger and more complicated ceramic structures. Thrown cylinders, bowls, and closed bottle, forms that are cut, scraped, and then re-shaped, make up to five-foot high sculptures. Raul Angulo Coronel, U.S.A.*

4. *The thrown form takes shapes that slabs or coils may have difficulty holding, as seen in "Quarter Horse," 40 inches long and 18 inches high. Raul Angulo Coronel. U.S.A.*

5. *Painting the surface of the greenware or bisque pot with a resist such as liquid wax or rubber latex and then applying a clay slip or a glaze over the design is a technique that often gives pleasant results. Patrick Kennedy, U.S.A.*

1

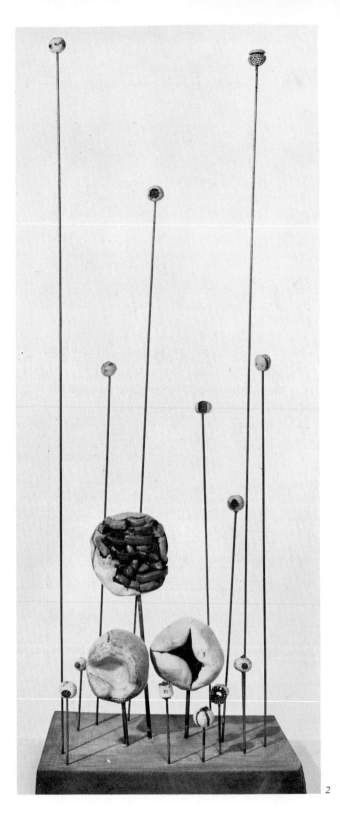

2

3

5

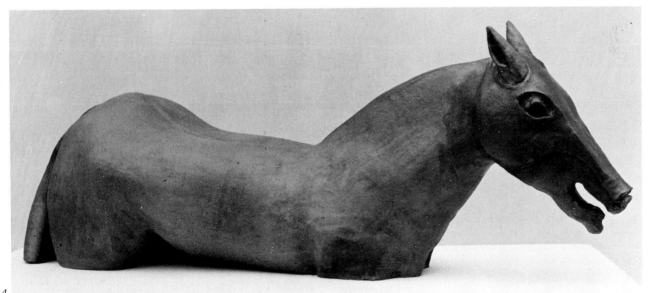

4

1. *This ten-inch sculptured vase has a pleasing
tactile quality. Marguerite Wildenhain, U.S.A.*
2. *Textures made by pressing into semi-moist
clay the end of a mop handle, a saw-toothed modeling tool,
the end of a Japanese brush, a common pencil, a nail head,
and the carved end of a wooden dowel.*

PART IV: Decoration

2

Whatever form of decoration is used in ceramics must relate to the shape and form of the item constructed. While the piece of ceramics is under construction, scraping, indenting, modeling and even beating, all help to make the form or the shape desired. The fingers leave their marks and the shape retains many "making" marks. Smoothing over the making marks often makes the piece of ceramics cold, stiff, and lifeless. These marks can easily be extended into general textural qualities. Every piece of ceramics has some form of *texture*, whether it be smooth or rough. The methods of obtaining texture are endless; however, there are a few that seem to be popular and are rather simple to obtain. Rolling clay over burlap will leave an overall texture that can be pleasing; scraping over the surface of heavily grogged clay will leave another interesting texture. Textures may be added by the use of such items as a sponge, a nail head, a saw-toothed tool, a modeling tool, an incised roller, a simple wooden or plaster stamp, wooden engraving tools, or a broken piece of wood. Finding objects that lend themselves to interesting textures often adds a sense of creativity that normally would not be present in

a certain piece of work. Textures can be applied when the slab is rolled out or after the construction is completed; however, the texture should be applied when the clay is soft enough to take the imprint, yet not so soft as to stick to the texturing device. The texture of certain functional items must be considered so that the problem of cleaning food particles is eliminated. A bowl, for example, should not have a rough texture on the inside. Textures should also not only be pleasant to the sight, but to the touch. Sharp, jagged edges are susceptible to being chipped and can cause cuts and scratches. While texturing is generally thought of as an overall pattern applied to the surface of a piece of ceramics, it can be applied in bands or on certain sections of a construction as well. The texture should add to and work with the entire statement of the form rather than overpower it. The form of the pot is the prime importance. Of course, there are many other forms of decoration besides texturing that can be utilized with a ceramic shape.

The use of the *brush* offers another wide variety of decorative approaches. A good medium-sized Japanese brush can serve the potter well, while other

1. Textures can be made by the fingers, by pressing a coil of clay with a modeling tool, with burlap, the end of a broken stick, and a folded band saw blade. The band saw blade is also a good tool for carving, scraping, and shaping the surface of a pot.
2. Textures made by the head of bolt, a nut, a wire loop tool, a bent piece of wire, a modeling tool, a heavy piece of cord, and some string wrapped around a flat stick.
3. Texture-patterns of the splintered end of a stick, a caster, corrugated cardboard, a plaster rasp, a saw-toothed, metal, flexible rib, and a piece of plastic packing material.

4. Clay textured with burlap offers a rough surface that can work well with or without a glaze. The application of a stain, engobe, or glaze generally accentuates the burlap texture.
5. A 19" high wheel-thrown bowl with a carved surface. Don Sutherland, U.S.A.

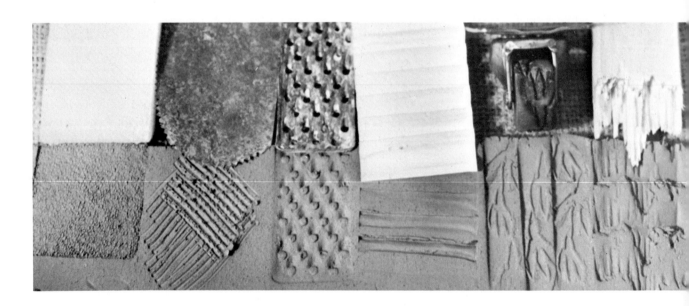

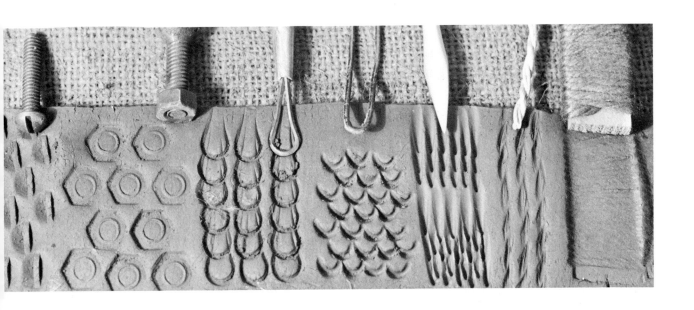

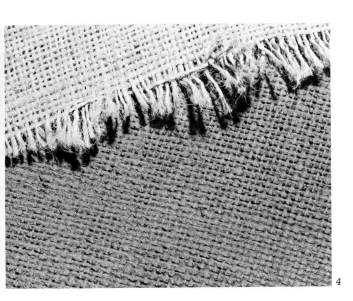

4

5

*Brushed decoration gives definition to the
ceramic forms created by June Black,
New Zealand.*

1

2

shapes are often used to meet specific requirements such as a flat brush for applying washes, a stubby brush for dabbing, or a small, coarse, straw-bristled brush for free slip application methods. Brushes can be used to apply bands of decoration as well as free-hand patterns or other art work. The brushed design should work with and further emphasize the form.

When a coloring oxide is added to a clay slip, the name used to describe this colored clay slip is *engobe*. Engobes have many uses especially in relation to decoration. Engobes are best applied to leatherhard clay; however, if the engobe and the clay body have a good fit and there is not a lot of shrinkage, engobes can be applied to bone dry ware. Engobes, in most instances, can be applied to bisque ware. Engobes can be applied with a brush, or if the entire surface of a form is to be covered, pouring or dipping the engobe gives better results.

A technique often used to advantage is the *sgraffito* method of decoration. A layer of engobe is applied to the surface of the ware, usually with a wide brush; and either while the engobe is still wet or after it dries, a design or decoration is scratched

through the engobe, allowing the clay body to show through. The scratching can be done with a pointed tool, a modeling tool, or any sharp instrument, depending upon the effect desired.

Clay can be *carved* into with any number of tools. The carving method is usually done while the clay is leatherhard; however, bone dry clay can be carved if care is taken.

Decoration can be applied in the form of little clay wads, clay coils, or other shapes of clay pressed to the semi-moist clay surface.

Pots can easily be *stamped* with carved bisque stamps, wooden, metal, rubber or plaster forms.

Slip trailing is yet another method of decoration that is quickly applied and is easy to do. A small ear syringe is the best tool for slip trailing. The bulb is filled with a liquid clay slip and the design is applied in linear form from the small opening of the syringe. The syringe is also used to apply slip or glazes in a very free, running fashion that usually relates well to most free ceramic forms.

Two other methods involving clay slip or engobe are *feather combing* and *slip combing*. Feather combing

1. This small bowl boasts the interesting effect of having the outside carved lines follow the inner contour. Dorothy W. Perkins, U.S.A.
2. The plate and open bowl form offer a favorable area on which to apply decoration. This large, shallow bowl is richly decorated by scratching into an applied engobe. Dora Pezic-Mijatovic, Yugoslavia.

and slip combing are normally used on flat bowls and plates. The surface is first covered with one slip and allowed to set until it becomes slightly settled or dull in finish. Then another contrasting slip is trailed over the form in close parallel lines. The form, when possible, should be resting flat on a board and formed into a bowl or plate shape after the decoration is applied. The clay slab, resting on the board, is then bumped on a table surface to cause the two engobes to blend slightly; the bottom engobe and the top engobe should be level. Then, with feather combing, a fine-pointed instrument such as a sharpened quill is lightly pulled across the surface, not into the slip, dragging the slips to form a pattern obtainable by no other method. With slip combing, a simple comb-like tool is dragged across the surface just as in the feather combing method. The end results depend upon the spacing of the teeth in the combed tool and the width of each individual tooth.

Marbling is still another effect that can be obtained by preparing the surface of the clay in the same way as in slip or feather combing, except that the slab of clay is moved around, shaken, or twisted to produce an accidental effect that resembles marble.

Once clay has been bisque fired, the use of commercially prepared *stains* can be adopted. Stains are simply oxides or a combination of oxides prepared to give specific colors usually under a glaze. Stains are best brushed on and not gone over a second time; they are made to hold without blurring. If stains are used over a glaze, a different effect is obtained; usually stronger colors and blurring occurs. Straight oxides, such as iron, chromium, manganese, copper, rutile, or cobalt, may also be used in much the same fashion as commercially prepared stains; however, straight oxides are coarse in texture and give harsher and less controllable colors. Stains may also be applied to greenware or over engobes.

GLAZES

Much can be done with the raw surface of clay and it can easily be considered a finished surface; how-

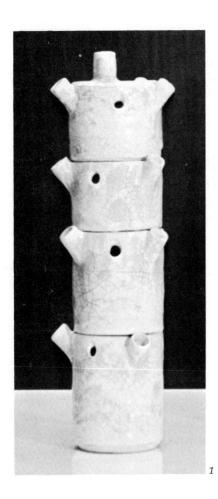

1

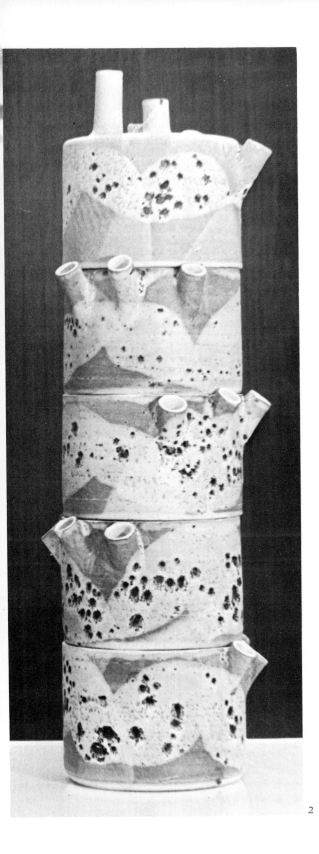

2

ever, just as a new piece of clothing can bring out a special beauty in the wearer, so can a glaze enhance a piece of ceramics.

There is no way of telling exactly just how glazes were discovered or even which people of the world first started using glazes; glazes are known to have been used in many pre-historic civilizations. Just as the discovery of firing clay was more than likely accidental, so was the discovery of early glazes. Man has always had concern with protecting and covering vulnerable items just as he clothed himself from the elements of wind, rain, and cold; and so it was the use of glazes that allowed a pot to hold water, withstand cleaning, and serve many functions.

A glaze may be defined as a mixture of certain earthy materials which, when applied to the surface of a ceramic body and subjected to heat of high temperature, melt in place to form a non-porous, glassy coating that can be of a specific color and texture.

Even though a glaze serves a utilitarian function, when considering ceramics as an art, a glaze should enhance, supplement, and otherwise work with the form. Glazes may be used to give a contrast in surface texture or color, create line, form, and space, or develop a design, drawing, or decoration.

The list of ingredients that make up a glaze is referred to as the glaze recipe and when the ingredients of a glaze recipe are mixed, the mixture is called a glaze batch. A glaze batch may be quite simple and contain only a few items or it may be quite complex and contain many materials.

The materials that go into a glaze are all in the form of oxides. Some commonly used glaze oxides are as follows:

(RO group)
Antimony Oxide — SbO
Barium Oxide — BaO
Boric Oxide — B_2O_3
Calcium Oxide — CaO
Lead Oxide — PbO
Lithium Oxide — Li_2O

1. *While the main body of this bottle is strongly decorated with a carved texture, only the neck and interior is glazed, adding interesting contrast between the two areas. Patrick Kennedy, U.S.A.*

2. *The carved texture strengthens the foot of this thrown and slabbed stoneware pot. Lyle N. Perkins, U.S.A.*

3. *When glaze is applied over a raised or carved line, it thins out or thickens up correspondingly, thus creating a change in its color and opacity. "Mask" plate. Zlata Radej, Yugoslavia.*

Magnesium Oxide — MgO
Potassium Oxide — K_2O
Sodium Oxide — Na_2O
Strontium Oxide — SrO
Zinc Oxide — ZnO
(R_2O_3 group)
Aluminum Oxide — Al_2O_3
Titanium Oxide — TiO_2
(RO_2 group)
Silicon Dioxide — SiO_2

The first group of oxides is used primarily as a flux, to cause the silica to melt. In the second group of oxides, alumina is used to make the glass stiffen and keep it from running off the vertical surface of ware. Very rarely is alumina left out of a glaze; but when it is, crystals form under proper firing conditions. The silica is the glass-forming agent of the glaze and is the bulk of all glazes. The other materials could be considered as modifiers. Because no two oxides react exactly alike, it is easy to imagine the endless variety of glazes that can be produced. The exact degree of temperature at which a glaze will melt depends upon the make-up of the glaze formula and how much fluxing power has been added in relation to the amount of silica. It is for this reason that one must be careful to fire a glazed piece to the precise temperature for which it calls. It is interesting to note that the base composition of a glaze is somewhat similar to that of clay. For that matter, some clays are used as glazes, such as Albany clay slip. The fluxing oxides also have uses other than promoting melting.

Antimony may be used as an opacifier and when combined with lead it is used to form Naples yellow in a glaze.

Barium is primarily used to produce mat glazes.

Boric oxide is a very good flux and is often used in place of lead. It should be used in an insoluble form as should all glaze materials and can be found in the mineral Colemanite.

Calcium is not only an excellent flux, but it contributes to the hardness and durability of a glaze.

Lead is an excellent flux and works quite well in low-fire situations. It is very trouble free and can produce beautiful effects. However, working with raw lead is dangerous when caution is not taken, as lead in its raw state is poisonous. If at all possible, lead should be used in a fritted form. A frit is any material mixed with a glass (silica), fired in a crucible, cooled, and ground into a powder. What happens is that the lead, in this case being a soluble material, is made insoluble and its toxic effect is reduced. Most commercially prepared glazes that use lead introduce it into the batch as a frit.

Lithium, because of its expense, is not commonly used. However, it is a good flux.

Magnesium is best used as a high-fire flux. It imparts a smooth, somewhat mat texture to high-fire ware.

Potassium and *Sodium* are quite similar, both producing fluxing action at a wide range of temperatures. Sodium is the most common of the two and gives brilliant colors to a glaze when metallic coloring oxides are added.

Strontium works something like calcium; however, it is more expensive than calcium and therefore is used very little.

Zinc is a useful flux at middle temperature ranges to the higher ranges and is often used to produce matness and dryness. It often helps in smoothing out troublesome glazes.

Silica is the principal material in all glazes. It is indispensable and is the glass-forming agent within a glaze.

Alumina serves many important functions in a glaze even though it is used in relatively small amounts. It helps keep the glaze from running off vertical surfaces, a feature called viscosity, the stiffness of the glaze. Alumina also prevents the glaze from recrystallization during the cooling process, thereby allowing the glaze to cool into a smooth, noncrystalline surface. Alumina adds to the strength and hardness of glazes and, if used in certain larger amounts, will lend opacity and matness to glazes.

1

1. *These handbuilt pieces take almost symbolic stature. Ruth Duckworth, U.S.A.*
2. *The surface quality of this stoneware sculpture is pulled together by a milky glaze, poured unevenly over the carved, stamped, and pressed area. Finn Lynggaard, Denmark. Den Permanente Collection.*

2

When mixing a glaze it is not always possible to use straight oxides. Oxides are found in many minerals; and, for that reason, if the potter is going to use raw materials which contain more than one oxide in varying amounts, he must know what each raw material contains.

Some common raw materials used in glaze making are as follows:

Clay, Feldspar, Flint, Barium Carbonate, Whiting, Dolomite, Colemanite, Talc, White Lead, Magnesium Carbonate, and Zinc Oxide.

Clay is the main source of aluminum oxide in glazes. Clay, also containing silica, adds to the glassy quality of the glaze and, depending upon the amount of iron and other impurities, gives varying colors.

Flint, a form of quartz, is the chief source of silica in a glaze.

Feldspar is used in a great many glazes, adding varying amounts of silica and alumina as well as some alkalines such as calcium, potassium, or sodium, singly or in combination. There are many different types of feldspars such as orthoclase, albite, spodumene, or anorthite; and each one has a specific chemical composition. Commercially, manufacturers mine feldspars and prepare them to have a uniform composition and give their blend a trade name, such as Clinchfield, Keystone, Peaksville, Kona F-4, Buckingham, and so on. A formula may be ac-

quired from the manufacturer to know just what are the specific ingredients of its prepared feldspar.

Whiting is used in glazes as the main source of calcium. It is often referred to as calcium carbonate.

Barium Carbonate is used to present barium oxide in a glaze.

Dolomite is used whenever calcium carbonate and magnesium carbonate are required in a glaze.

Colemanite is used in glazes mainly because it contains boron in a near insoluble form. It also contains calcium.

Talc contains both silica and magnesia and small amounts of calcium. It is useful in reducing the maturing temperature of clay bodies.

White Lead is the best type of lead to be used in glazes as it is insoluble in water, free from impurities, and fine in particle size.

Magnesium Carbonate is the main source of magnesium oxide when used in a glaze.

Zinc Oxide is the only source of zinc in glazes. Because raw zinc may cause glaze flaws, it is best used in calcined form.

TYPES OF GLAZES
As man has always been interested in variety, he has developed a great many different glazes. Most glazes fall into certain categories or types.

A low-temperature glaze is any glaze that matures below 2000 degrees Fahrenheit, or cone 02. Low-temperature glazes are generally glassy, soft, and impart crazing; however, they can give a wide variety of colors that higher-fired glazes cannot, such as brilliant reds and oranges. There are two types of low-temperature glazes: low-temperature alkaline glazes and lead glazes. Lead glazes may also be fired as high as the middle ranges or to about cone 6.

A type of glaze that was developed in England to replace the poisonous nature of raw lead is the *Bristol glaze,* which is a middle-temperature glaze. Bristol glazes mature between cones 2 and 6. Glazes that are fired at about cone 7 and higher are considered either *porcelain* or *stoneware glazes.* The high-fired glazes are usually simpler than the lower-melting glazes and employ feldspar as a prominent ingredient. Even though brilliant color is not common in high-fired glazes, the artistic qualities found within the subtle, earthy tones (as well as the practicality of having a dense, durable surface) are definite advantages that should not be overlooked.

GLAZE TEXTURES
Glazes can be either transparent or opaque, bright or mat.

Transparent glazes, or clear glazes, are glazes that have been fired to maturity with all the components fusing completely. Transparency is considered to be a normal reaction to a complete firing. Just the opposite is true of many *opaque glazes,* as all the components are not completely fused and thus form a cloudy or muddy effect. Opacity is often desired and is not only obtained by underfiring, but can be achieved by adding certain ingredients such as tin oxide or zirconium. There are many other ways to produce an opaque or semi-opaque texture in a glaze, and the potter has but to experiment. If the surface of the glaze has a shine, it is considered a *bright glaze.* Bright glazes are glazes that are completely melted. A bright glaze may be either trans-

"Branch Form," 24 inch wheel and slab stoneware construction with carved clay additions. Maurice K. Grossman, U.S.A.

parent or opaque. The opposite of a bright glaze is a *mat glaze*. The quality of matness is usually quite pleasing artistically and unusually, because of its lack of highlights or brightness, displays the form of the pot better than a bright glaze. The textural surface of a mat glaze is normally pleasant to the touch; however, a disadvantage lies in the fact that mat surfaces are difficult to clean and for that reason are not practical for dinnerware or other utilitarian purposes. A mat glaze must always be opaque, as the very structure of a mat glaze does not permit light to pass through it. However, some glazes are semi-mat and allow enough light to pass through, giving a very pleasing effect over applied decoration, clay textures, or engobes. Semi-mat glazes are difficult to control and are not common on the commercial market. Mat glazes can be produced by adding a little barium oxide or clay to the base glaze. Under-fired glazes have the tendency to be mat or somewhat rough in texture.

GLAZE COLORS

A piece of ceramics not only has its three dimensions, its form and line, its texture, its sense of balance and life, but it also has color. How the color is to be obtained must be considered by the potter. Color may come from the clay body, from clay slips or engobes, from stains, or be added as metallic oxides to the glaze body itself. As a source of color in glazes, the metallic oxides are a chief contributor. The most commonly used metallic oxides for coloring glazes are as follows: Iron oxide, cobalt oxide, copper oxide, manganese oxide, chromium oxide, nickel oxide, rutile, ilmenite, vanadium oxide, and cadmium. Depending upon the type of base glaze, the firing temperature and conditions, each oxide will give certain colors. For example, if copper oxide is used with a low-temperature alkaline glaze, it will produce a turquoise color; if it is used with a lead glaze, it will produce a more green color; and if copper is used in a high-fire glaze in a reduction atmosphere, it may produce a dark burgundy red or ox-blood color. The amount of oxide present in the glaze generally produces differences in color. An over-abundance of most oxides will produce a metallic effect, which normally is rough and dull in appearance; however, a large amount of copper, about 16% under certain reduction conditions, can produce a true metallic copper.

Iron oxide is the most useful and most important coloring oxide. It usually produces earthy browns, but can produce pinks, greens, and blacks. Iron is often used with other oxides to make the color warmer and more earthy looking. Iron can be used in percentages up to 10 percent with success. *Cobalt oxide* is the most stable of the coloring oxides. It will always reflect the color blue. Because of its stability, it is wise to use it in relatively small amounts from about one-half of one percent to one percent. Cobalt often produces a very harsh blue and should be toned down with other oxides such as iron or manganese. *Copper oxide* is an excellent oxide used to produce blues and blue-greens. It is usually mixed in amounts from 2 to 5 percent. Under proper reduction firings, copper can produce a very handsome copper-red, ox-blood, flambé, or peach bloom color. *Manganese oxide* is a very satisfactory glaze colorant for purples or browns. It is normally used as manganese carbonate, but to the artist it has interesting spotting, speckling, or mottling effects when used as manganese dioxide. Manganese probably gives much richer shades of brown than iron when used in high-temperature glazes. In lower temperatures, it gives a very handsome deep purple when a small amount of cobalt is added. *Chromium oxide* is the most versatile of the glaze colorants, yielding such colors as yellow, pink, brown, green, or even reds, depending upon the base glaze and the firing conditions. Chromium is a good oxide to experiment with as the end results are not always predictable. *Nickel oxide* usually gives browns, but it, too, can give quite a variety of colors. It is often used to modify other colors. *Rutile* is a mineral which contains iron and titanium. It can give a pleasant brown or tan, but when used in granular form can produce

1. *A series of cylindrical shapes are*
excellently composed in this ceramic structure
that might be utilized as a candle holder.
Beate Kuhn, Germany.
2. *Ceramics as a mosaic form is used to form*
plates. Mira Keler, Yugoslavia.

1

2

a handsome mottled color, and for that reason is often added to other glaze colorants just for the rich surface texture that can be achieved. *Ilmenite* is another ore, just as rutile, that contains iron and titanium; however, it is cruder in form and produces dark specs in a glaze when admitted in its granular state. *Vanadium oxide* is the chief oxide in producing the color of yellow in glazes. It is best used as a stain and is relatively weak, requiring eight to ten percent to produce a strong yellow. *Cadmium*, when combined with selenium in a glaze stain and added to a low-fired, fritted glaze, gives red colors. Red is the most difficult color to get in glazing, and bright reds are almost an impossibility in high-fire ceramics. It is best to utilize a commercially prepared glaze and follow the manufacturer's suggestions as to application and firing in order to obtain a red-colored glaze. Red glazes tend to "burn out" easily and should be cooled rapidly in the firing process to prevent the color from disappearing.

GLAZE MIXING

When preparing a glaze from the raw materials, certain precautions must be taken. All glaze materials are not the same consistency, nor do they mix together alike. The glaze batch must first be weighed out in dry form on a small balance or scale. It is important to be exact, especially when measuring out small batches. Understand the scale and be sure it is balanced, clean, and in good working order. The dry batch, once it is weighed out, may be mixed with water. The water should be added slowly, and the mixture should be squeezed together well between the fingers until it is a smooth, paste-like consistency. Then more water can be added until the glaze is about the consistency of light cream. If there are ingredients within the glaze that do not mix well, or if they are not finely ground, a screen sieve of about 100 mesh should be used. Some glazes take in more water than others, and the amount of water necessary to get it the right consistency depends upon the glaze ingredients. In order to produce a smooth, uniform glaze, a *ball mill* may be employed. A ball mill is any container which can be closed tightly, rotated on some form of roller system, and which contains a certain amount of rounded pebbles. The glaze is placed inside the jar with water and the pebbles; and as the jar is rotated, the pebbles grind the glaze materials into a very fine and smooth mixture. The speed of the ball mill must be controlled, as too fast a motion will not allow the pebbles (or porcelain balls) to grind the glaze materials against the inside surface of the jar.

1

1. *An interesting contrast of form is seen in pots of the following potters: Sures, Grove, Markson, Hatfield, Drahanchuk, and Tillapaugh, all of Canada.*
2. *Close-up of clay in mosaic form.*
3. *The space need not be large nor the materials fancy to produce an effective glaze with a wide range of color possibilities. Glaze materials are inexpensive and mixing can be done by hand.*
4. *The balance scale is essential in glaze mixing. Each item must be weighed exactly according to the glaze recipe. If one ingredient will not fit easily on the scale, a container must be used. The added weight of the container must be compensated for on the other side of the scale.*
5. *Under normal cooling conditions, a glaze remains non-crystalline; however, with a drastic reduction of alumina in the glaze, it will form crystals as it cools. Because alumina is vital in maintaining viscosity, the crystalline glaze will run quite a bit and precautions must be taken to collect the glaze that runs off the surface of the pot, while the base of the pot must be ground smooth with a grinding wheel. The end effect of the crystalline glaze also produces "happy accidents," but in a different vein than does the raku process. This thrown porcelain bottle, with transparent brown-blue crystals, is a striking example of what crystals can do for a pot. Marc Hansen, U.S.A.*

3

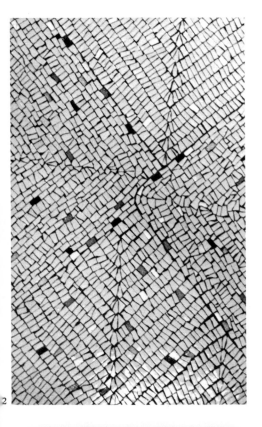

1

2

1. The surface of these small, thrown pots has a quality of freedom obtained by the raku method of production in which the brushed engobes and applied glaze, coupled with the firing method, create what is known as "happy accidents," by the author.

2. When tiny cracks appear in the surface of the glaze, the texture may be desirable and the technique is called a crackle glaze. If the effect is not desirable and is distracting to the pot, it is called crazing. In the case of this pitcher, the effect is controlled and creates a pleasant feeling. Dora Pezic-Mijatovic, Yugoslavia.

3. The texture of this six inch lidded bowl was added by applying a stiff clay slip with the finger tips. Dorothy W. Perkins, U.S.A.

4. The introduction of a high metallic oxide may produce lustrous specks known as an oilspot glaze. This 14 inch high bottle, fired to cone 10 in an electric kiln, has oilspots on a chartreuse glaze. Adrian Shaw, U.S.A.

5. A controlled oilspot produces a cratered decoration that works well with this 8 inch bowl. The overall texture is smooth and pleasing to the touch. Adrian Shaw, U.S.A.

6. A smooth, bright glaze of earthy colors enhances these three covered pots. Alessio Tasca, Italy.

3

4

5

6

*The use of two glazes of different textural
qualities more strongly suggest the form of
this 14 inch high, earthenware, "Mandrill
Baboon." Paul Bogatay, U.S.A.*

METHODS OF APPLYING GLAZES

Basically, there are four methods of applying a glaze: brushing, pouring, dipping, and spraying. The method of glaze application depends upon such factors as the type of glaze being used, the area on which the glaze is to be applied, and the end effect desired. When a glaze is to be applied to an area that is difficult to reach by any other method except brushing, then the brush must be used. However, brushing on a glaze is probably the most difficult method of glaze application with which to get an even coating. It is time-consuming, and is not the easiest method for interior surfaces. One important feature of glazing by brush is control. The glaze can be applied with a greater degree of accuracy. Brushing a glaze decoration over another glaze is acceptable and can be quite handsome. In this sense, when the glaze is used as a form of free-brush decoration, a design, or pattern, the brushing method is acceptable. The brush can also be utilized in applying glaze to small areas or areas that have been chipped and require repairing.

Pouring the glaze over the pot or into the pot is an excellent method of glaze application. It allows the glaze to run smoothly over the surface of the ceramics and is a very quick method of glazing. When glazing a pot, it is best to pour the glaze inside first, about three-fourths full, and then slowly pour it back out while revolving the pot to ensure an even application throughout the interior surface. The longer the glaze is allowed to remain inside the pot before it is poured out again, the thicker the application. The outside surface should be glazed last by holding the piece of ceramics upside down and slowly pouring the glaze over the surface. A small ear syringe is an excellent tool that may be used to squirt the glaze over the surface of a pot. The syringe can be used to apply different forms of decoration to the surface of the pot, also. The consistency of the glaze must be thick enough to develop an application that will cover as intended. The fired piece will reflect the proper thickness of application.

Dipping a form into glaze is an excellent way to get an all over, even application. The problems that may arise can only be attributed to the lack of enough glaze and the proper size container. Tilting a bowl shape into a glaze can give an interesting pattern. If the open end of a pot is dipped directly into the glaze, the air pocket trapped inside will keep the glaze from penetrating the already glazed interior.

Glazes can be *sprayed* onto the surface of ware. The spraying method requires the use of a compressor, spray gun, and spray booth, at a slight initial cost. Much glaze is lost as it is being sprayed, and getting a proper application may be difficult at first. Some of the glaze that forms in the back of the spray booth can be scraped together and re-used, often producing an interesting effect, usually dark in color.

It may be desirous to obtain a detailed pattern of different colored glazes on the surface of a pot with more control than pouring or dipping can give. If this is the case, spraying the pot with a glaze over stencils is the method to use.

When a good deal of control is required, *brushing* the glaze on the pot is probably the best answer. The difficulty of using a brush is getting an even glaze of correct thickness. The glaze should be applied with a light touch, allowing the glaze to run off the brush smoothly. If the brush is pressed downward with too much pressure, an uneven application will result. The type of brush used in applying a glaze should be soft and large enough to carry a good amount of glaze. Special effects can be obtained by using a stiff brush, or even a small straw broom if the glaze is compatible. Utilization of the brush in a satisfactory manner requires experience, but once it has been mastered, striking effects can be achieved.

4

1. *Dipping a pot into glaze. This method of glazing is very quick and effective; however, the quantity of glaze required, the size and shape of the pot to be glazed, and the container in which the pot is to be dipped, must all be considered.*
2. *When dipping is impractical, pouring the glaze over the surface of the pot can produce excellent results. The use of a small syringe for glaze application offers greater control.*
3. *Applying a glaze to the interior of a pot. The glazed area is impervious to water; and while it may not be visible inside bottles and other type forms, the pot will fire more successfully with glaze on both inside and outside surfaces.*
4. *"Cosas #2," a five foot high ceramic form constructed from thrown units flattened and attached. The surface was glazed in blue-grey, white, and umber, making use of cut-out paper forms as shapes in a negative stencil-like technique. Albert C. Parvin Company, by Raul Angulo Coronel, U.S.A.*

1. A simulated view of the bisque stacking indicating the placement of the kiln shelf over the first layer of pots.

2. A typical bisque stacking for a small, top-loading kiln. Notice the placement of the pyrometric cones so that they can be readily seen through the peep hole.

3. Standard pyrometric cones placed in a plastic pad of clay are the best determinants of the temperature of a clay body and glaze during a kiln firing. Punching small openings in the cone pad is a recommended practice which helps prevent the pad from blowing up in the firing. The cone on the right side of the clay pad will melt first. The smaller cones are used in conjunction with kiln guards (automatic safety devices) in electric kilns.

1

PART V: Firing

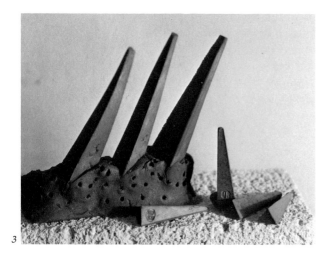

3

FIRING THE KILN

When clay is subjected to red-hot temperatures, a chemical and physical change takes place that turns it from a porous, plastic, and brittle state to a non-porous, vitreous, dense material which has such permanence that it has been a major contribution in revealing the history of ancient civilizations.

All the effort of preparing clay, wedging, creating, constructing, and decorating means nothing until the process has been completed with a successfully fired kiln.

TYPES OF KILNS

Two major types of kilns are *fuel-burning* kilns and *electric* kilns. Fuel-burning kilns can be wood, coal, oil, charcoal, or gas-burning. The gas-burning kiln is more common than other types of fuel-burning kilns. Gas kilns are relatively cheap to fire; however, they are bulky, require a chimney, and need more attention in firing than electric kilns. The advantages of having a gas kiln, other than economy, is that there is much more variety in the surface of the glaze as well as the clay body, the colors are warmer and richer, and the texture is much more lively. This is due to the atmospheric conditions within the fuel-burning kiln. Both the clay body and the glazed surface of pots fired in fuel-burning atmospheres

tend to develop artistic innuendos that give depth and become an intricate part of the entire ceramic concept.

Fuel-burning kilns can be classified up-draught or down-draught, according to the direction in which the draught travels. Whenever a fuel burns, oxygen must be present. All fuel-burning kilns must have some way of getting a continuous supply of air into the kiln chamber in order to have combustion. Generally, the burners, placed at the bottom of the kiln, can be adjusted to allow the exact amount of air to enter with the fuel for the most efficient burning. The stack, or chimney, must be designed so that it creates a draught which will pull the air into the kiln and also keep the flame burning within the kiln. In the case of an up-draught kiln, the rising heat which enters at the bottom of the kiln is simply allowed to continue up and out the top of the kiln. Small fuel-burning kilns are normally up-draught kilns because an even distribution of the temperature is easier to maintain in a small area. However, when the inside dimensions of a kiln are larger than approximately three feet high, the temperature can vary from top to bottom enough to cause firing problems. The down-draught kiln gives more even heat distribution within the kiln. The flame enters

91

Normally, in fuel burning kilns, the flame does not come into direct contact with the ware. Usually, the flame is directed around the ware by muffle walls. If the flame is not allowed to burn directly into the kiln chamber and if there is sufficient oxygen present for complete combustion, the atmosphere is kept clear of any burning residue that can affect the clay body and the glaze. This type of firing is called an *oxidation firing*. Any fuel-burning kiln that has muffle walls (sometimes called baffle walls) is referred to as a *muffle kiln*.

If, on the other hand, the flame is allowed to enter the kiln chamber and if the oxygen is not sufficient for complete combustion, free carbon (black smoke), plus carbon monoxide, fills the kiln. The carbon is still active and is searching for oxygen. The oxygen within the clay body and especially within the glaze is attacked by the free carbon which in turn affects the color of the clay body and glaze. This reaction is called *reduction firing*. Many potters prefer to fire in a reduction atmosphere so that the finished effect on the ware is warm, earthy, and pleasing in texture, even though the color range of reduction firing is limited. Reduction firing should be thought of as an incomplete-burning fire in contrast to a clean-burning oxidizing fire that accompanies an efficient kiln firing.

Electric kilns, since they burn no fuel and are normally equipped with simple controls and safety features, are the easiest to fire. The kiln atmosphere is considered to be neutral in an electric kiln. This type of atmosphere leaves most glazes flat and plain without the depth that other types of kiln firings can give. Because there is no flue or chimney in the electric kiln, the water vapor that is driven off the ware in the early stages of firing should be allowed to escape by propping the door open slightly for the first hour or so of firing.

Even though the basic firing principles for all kilns

from the bottom of the down-draught kiln as usual; however, as the heat rises, there is no outlet at the top of the kiln. The heat is then forced back down the center to the bottom again where a narrow trough or flue draws the heat out the back of the kiln and finally up the chimney. The draught is usually more difficult to develop in a down-draught kiln, but a fairly even temperature can be obtained, which is the important point to consider. Some down-draught kilns have a fan system built into the flue area in order to maintain a constant pull of air through the kiln.

The puffed up form of this 38 inch high bud vase compliments its title, "Obese Object." The impressed lines which run diagonally around the pot appear to contain the growing form. It is almost as though the form will not be held by the lines, and it invites the viewer's attention who feels compelled to see the form before it bursts. Eugene Friley, U.S.A.

are the same, the physical structure of the kiln varies from situation to situation, from culture to culture. A very crude, but effective, method of firing low-maturing ware is the *bonfire*. The ware is stacked over a huge pile of dried branches and wood, the fire is started, and the flame is continually fed with bundles of dry branches or grass. There are a lot of seconds with this method: however, a great many pieces can be fired at one time because there is no space problem that the interior of a normal kiln presents.

Kilns can be built into or onto the bank of a hill, thus utilizing natural insulation and the rising heat. The *climbing kilns* of Japan and other oriental areas are basically a series of kiln chambers built on a hillside and connected so that the heat originating at the bottom is taken full advantage of in each succeeding chamber. In large, commercial ceramic plants, the *tunnel kiln* expedites the firing process. The ware is stacked on a slowly moving belt that rotates into the kiln chamber where the temperature is regulated in order to fire the ware normally. By the time the ware comes out of the long tunnel, it has been cooled enough for packing and shipment.

Because of the physical structure of some kilns, placing the ware inside can be a problem. A solution for such instances is to have the ware stacked outside the kiln on a platform which can be rolled on tracks into the kiln chamber. Doors for large kilns can be attached to an overhead winch and lifted into place. The potter must know his needs, allowing for future expansion and changes, and choose the type of kiln accordingly.

Some kilns are not always easy to construct. However, it takes very little effort to build and successfully fire a small, up-draught, low-fire kiln. The Japanese were innovators of a type of ware that is fired in such a simple kiln. The ware and the unique firing process is known as *raku*.

RAKU FIRING

Because of the quick, direct, and simple raku process, the entire concept of firing a kiln can easily be understood. The raku process is an excellent method in teaching firing procedures; it takes the mystery out of firing a kiln.

The kiln can easily be constructed from fire bricks and the heat can be introduced either by burning charcoal or wood or by burning bottled gas. The flame should enter at the bottom of the kiln and should be directed toward some sort of baffling device such as a fire brick, around a kiln shelf, up and out a small flue opening at the top. The kiln is brought to maturing temperature quickly *before* any ware is placed inside. The clay body for raku ware must be very open, usually containing a great deal of fire clay and grog, so that it can withstand thermal shock. Once the temperature of the kiln is high enough, usually about 1800° F., the door is unbricked and the ware, previously bisqued with glaze applied, is placed inside. Gloves and a pair of long, metal tongs are used to prevent the hands from getting burned. The ware is observed through the flue opening, or a peephole. When the glaze on the ware begins to melt and becomes shiny, the pots are taken out with the tongs and dunked directly into a large container of cold water. Because of the type of clay body, the ware is able to withstand the abrupt change of temperature. Quite often, before placing the ware directly into the water, it is rolled in a combustible material such as sawdust, paper, dry grass, or leaves. The red-hot pot causes the sawdust or other material to burn, which reduces the surface area. The color of the glaze is altered in much the same fashion as it is in a reduction firing. The material that burns on the pot not only affects the color, but forms a textural pattern as well. Leaves are sometimes used to get interesting patterns. Good raku ware displays a free, quick, spontaneous character in its method of construction, glaze application, and firing process.

1

1. The foundation of the raku kiln is constructed with fire bricks and then covered with a layer of sand for greater insulation.

2. The walls of the kiln are built. Notice the small opening near the bottom which will serve as the heat inlet.

3. The top layer of bricks is tapered inward to provide a more stable support for the kiln shelf which will cover the top. Calking up any cracks in the kiln wall with a groggy clay helps to insulate the kiln.

4. The raku kiln is complete. The door is bricked shut. In this instance, the heat is supplied from a propane gas tank through a make-shift burner.

5. After the kiln is heated to red-hot temperature, the door is unbricked and the ware is inserted. When the glaze appears to be mature, the pot is taken from the kiln while it is still red-hot. About twenty to thirty minutes is an average time for ware to remain inside the kiln.

6. The form may be turned or rolled in sawdust which burns over the surface of the pot, causing a reduction effect. The flaming pot is then quickly dumped into a can of cold water.

7. Even though a small kiln is used, a great number of pots can be fired in a relatively short time.

4

7

MEASURING AND MANAGING THE KILN TEMPERATURE

The temperature within the kiln can be measured a number of ways. Many potters are able to tell the temperature by the color of the fire. As the kiln gets hot, the fire changes from deep cherry red to near white heat. Two common instruments used to measure kiln temperatures are *pyrometric cones* and *pyrometers*. Pyrometric cones are small pieces of clay with fluxes added to allow them to melt at known temperatures. A number is stamped on the side of each cone indicating the temperature at which it will melt. Cones are normally placed in groups of three, one which will melt slightly before the desired temperature, the center one which will melt exactly at the desired temperature, and the third one which would indicate any slight overfiring. The cones are placed in a small wad of fire clay or groggy clay known as a cone pad, and set inside the kiln directly in front of a small opening in the kiln called a peep hole. The cones should be tilted slightly so that it will be apparent when they begin to slump over and melt. As an example, if the kiln is to be fired to 1830° Fahrenheit, cone number 06, the first cone placed in the clay pad would be cone 07.

A view of some greenware placed in the bottom of an electric kiln.

Cone 07 will melt first as a warning that the desired temperature is about 20 to 30 minutes away at a normal firing rate. Cone 06, the middle cone, is placed to the left of cone 07. When the middle cone slumps over, the kiln should be turned off and all dampers closed tightly. The cone on the left, 05, is simply used to give some indication of possible overfiring. The pyrometric cone measures the temperature of the glaze or clay body.

The pyrometer measures the temperature of the kiln atmosphere, and, therefore, is not quite as accurate as cones. However, the pyrometer, a mechanical device that works as a large thermometer, can be very useful in gauging the temperature increase rate. Most electric kilns are equipped with pyrometers. The pyrometer can be attached to an automatic cut-off system as a safety measure against over-firing. Some electric kilns have a small attachment which accepts a smaller version of the pyrometric cone; and when the cone melts, the kiln is automatically shut off. This device is sometimes referred to as a kiln guard. The burner systems on fuel burning kilns can also be rigged with safety devices.

What takes place within the kiln during the firing governs the management of the firing cycle. The first change that takes place during the firing is complete drying of the clay. The atmospheric water must be driven off slowly, otherwise steam will form within the clay body and, expanding and finding no way out, will cause the pot to explode. Thick-walled pots or forms with heavy cross-sections are more likely to explode than thinner-walled shapes.

At about 660° Fahrenheit the chemically combined water begins to be driven off. The same results can happen during this stage of firing as in the first stage if the kiln is fired too rapidly. Eventually, the clay becomes completely dehydrated. Later, as the temperatures reach red-heat, the clay begins to vitrify, to harden up, tighten, and glassify. The object is to fire the clay to the point when it is at its greatest level of vitrification, before it slumps or melts. When clay and glazes reach this stage they are called mature. Each clay body and glaze has its own point of maturity. The secret to successful firing lies in slow, even firings with slow, even cooling. The temperature in most kilns should not be increased more rapidly than 50 to 100 degrees Fahrenheit per hour in the initial stages and 100 to 200 degrees per hour in the later stages. Once the desired temperature has been reached in glaze firings, the kiln should be maintained at that level for at least one-half hour.

This procedure of maintaining the temperature is called soaking the kiln and allows time for the glaze to settle and smooth out. With electric kilns, each band should be turned on low until the temperature has passed the stage of dehydration. Then the kiln may be turned up to medium for a few hours before it is turned up to high. Electric kilns can be soaked by turning them down to medium for a while after they have reached the maturing temperature. With gas kilns, the temperature is easily maintained at a constant point by turning the valves down low. It is extremely important to close up the kiln completely once it has been turned off. Too rapid cooling could cause every piece of ceramics within the kiln to blow up due to the abrupt contraction of the clay and glazes as it passes from red-hot to cool temperatures. The damper, which is used to regulate the amount of draught through the flue, must be closed as well as the peep holes and oxygen intakes, which are normally at the head of each burner.

STACKING THE BISQUE KILN

Because no glaze is applied to the pots in a bisque firing, the ware can be stacked very tightly and pieces can be nested one inside the other. The pieces can be placed on the kiln floor, and on shelves made of highly refractory clay. The shelves are supported by posts, also made of clay. Anything placed inside the kiln to facilitate the stacking of ware, such as shelves, posts, or pins, is called kiln furniture. Kiln furniture aids the potter in taking full advantage of the space within the kiln.

Bone dry ware must be handled with caution as it is quite delicate. However, with proper nesting, many pots can be stacked within the kiln.

FIRING THE BISQUE KILN

In most instances, the ceramic form should undergo two separate firings, a bisque firing and a glaze firing. The bisque firing is a preliminary firing which prepares the clay for easier handling when the glaze is to be applied, and proves the form so that seconds and blown pots are eliminated in the final stage. The bisque firing is fired lower in temperature than the final glaze firing which keeps the clay body open enough to accept a glaze (and other forms of decoration) more easily. If the pot is glazed and fired all in one operation, the possibility of explosions increases. When a glazed piece blows up in the kiln, the many fragments attach themselves to other pots as well as the kiln wall, ceiling, and floor. Usually, in a bisque firing, if one pot explodes, it causes no harm to other pots or the kiln.

The first phase of stacking a bisque kiln which simulates how the ware should be placed inside the kiln.

97

Contrasting textures tell the story of this thrown cylinder, paddled, cut, and rejoined. A natural and black clay body, 36 inch high form, titled "Woman." Raul Angulo Coronel, U.S.A.

STACKING THE GLAZE KILN

Placing glazed ware in the kiln must be done with care so that the raw glaze is not marred or chipped from the pot. The kiln should be brushed clear of debris and the kiln shelves must be coated with a layer of kiln wash, equal parts of flint and kaolin mixed with water to a thick paint consistency. Kiln wash aids in preventing ware from sticking to the shelf. Glazed pots must not touch each other during the firing or they will be fused together, and separating them is often impossible without breakage. About one-eighth of an inch space should be allowed between pieces, kiln furniture, and kiln walls. The bottoms of ware should not be glazed; and, if the glaze is known to run a bit, the application should stop approximately one-fourth of an inch from the bottom. If shelves are placed on three props, there is less tendency for wobbling. However, if four supports are necessary and a wobble develops, a wad of heavily grogged clay or fire clay should be inserted between the shelf and support. Once the kiln is stacked, the pyrometric cones enclosed, and the door shut or bricked up, the kiln is ready for firing.

FIRING THE GLAZE KILN

Because there is a minimum of drying or dehydration in glaze firing, the early stages can proceed quite rapidly. Soon the kiln reaches red-hot temperatures and the glaze begins to fuse. The early fusing is called sintering. Later, usually several cones below maturing temperature, the glaze starts to melt. As it melts, it may even bubble up and "boil" on the surface of the pot. As the glaze matures, the bubbles disappear. If the kiln is shut off too soon, it is possible to catch the bubbles before they have a chance to smooth out. The end result is that craters, pits, or pinholes cover the surface of the pot. The glaze kiln should be allowed to soak once it has reached maturity.

If the kiln is a fuel-burning one, it may be desirous to reduce the glaze. The actual time that the atmosphere is reduced during the firing cycle is only about one hour. The rest of the firing time is oxidation firing. It is advisable to reduce the kiln at two different times. The first time should be when the clay body will best react to the free carbon, turning it darker in color and richer in texture. With most clays, reduction should begin at about 1450° Fahrenheit. A reduction time of only one-half hour is all that is necessary. When the first cone begins to bend, the kiln may be reduced for the final time. Because with reduction the fire is not burning at its highest point of efficiency, the kiln will not go up very rapidly. Nevertheless, it is important to keep the kiln temperature rising quite slowly during the last stages of reduction firing. Once the cones are down, the final soaking period must take place in oxidation. When reduction takes place, the flame from within the kiln will appear at the peephole and make viewing the cones difficult. By blowing at the peephole and quickly looking into the kiln, the cones can be readily viewed during the reduction period of firing. The greater degree of reduction, the more smoke is developed and the more flame will appear at any slight opening in the kiln. A moderate degree of reduction is all that is necessary in most reduction firings.

Electric kilns may be reduced by placing anything that burns into the peephole. Wood chips or even moth balls will give similar effects of a fuel-burning reduction firing. The problem with reducing electric kilns is that the elements within the kiln can be damaged heavily by the free carbon, and the life of the kiln is shortened considerably. The same effect may be obtained without reducing the kiln by adding one to two percent silicon carbide to the glaze recipe. This method of "false" reduction never gives true reduction results; however, the addition of silicon carbide may tend to more completely develop a glaze effect that is difficult to achieve even under normal reduction firing methods.

MENDING BROKEN FIRED WARE

In most cases, broken ware is too difficult to repair. However, in certain instances, where whole sections break apart and can be set together without falling apart, a coating of glaze can be applied to the separated areas as a glue. The piece can be fired; and, with luck, the glaze will fuse the two pieces together. Small cracks can be filled after the final firing with any number of permanent drying materials such as wood fillers, acrylics, or putties. Most repaired areas are easy to detect, and time should not be wasted trying to fix them; rather start over again remembering what caused the problem in the previous work.

Only by skilled manipulation of the clay and glaze has the potter achieved a true sense of spontaneity. The faces were made from press molds and attached to very plastic thrown forms. Coille Hooven, U.S.A.

CERAMIC TERMS

Absorption: soaking up water.

Acid: one of three types of chemicals which make up a glaze. The most important acid is silica.

Aeolian: carried by the wind.

Agateware: ceramics that has been wedged or decorated to resemble agate.

Air floated: separated by air to make particles of similar size.

Albany slip: a natural clay which melts at cone 8 to a dark brown color, used as a glaze on clay when fired at a higher temperature.

Alkali: any material having definite basic properties. In ceramics the term refers to compounds of potassium and sodium which act as fluxes in alkaline glazes.

Alumina: a major ingredient found in all clays and most glazes. It is the chief oxide in the neutral group. It gives greater strength to clay bodies and glazes. It is quite important in lending viscosity to glazes and it aids in the formation of mat glazes.

Ash: the residue of burnt wood, leaves, grass, seaweed, and so forth. It normally contains from 40 to 75 per cent silica, from 5 to 15 per cent alumina and smaller amounts of iron, phosphorus, lime, potash, and magnesia, which provides the bulk of a high-temperature glaze batch.

Aventurine: a glaze compound of a lead, soda, or boric oxide flux with usually an excess of iron oxide. With slow cooling, iron crystals form which sparkle underneath the glaze surface.

Bag wall: a baffle wall which separates the kiln chamber from the combustion area.

Ball clay: a very fine-grained, secondary clay with a high degree of plasticity which fires nearly white in color even though it contains considerable organic matter. It is often added to a clay body to increase plasticity.

Ball mill: a porcelain jar filled with rounded flint pebbles and rotated slowly to blend and grind glaze ingredients.

Banding wheel: a turntable on which work may be rotated while it is shaped or decorated. (Also known as a twirler, whirler, or decorating wheel.)

Bat: any slab or disk made of wood or Plaster of Paris on which pottery is formed or dried. The plaster bat is also used to remove or absorb excess water from clay.

Batch: a measured or weighed mixture of materials such as a glaze batch, a batch of clay, or a batch for an engobe.

Bentonite: an extremely plastic clay of volcanic origin. It is used to increase plasticity in clay bodies and must be mixed with other ingredients in dry form before it can be used.

Binders: any material such as gums, polyvinyl alcohol, or methylcellulose used to increase glaze adherence to the clay surface or to give added strength to a cast or pressed clay body. Gum tragacanth and gum arabic are natural gums. Synthetic gums are practical because they do not sour.

Bisque or bisquit: ware that has been fired, but not glazed. A bisque firing is normally a low firing of about cone 07 or 06.

Blow-hole: a small opening at the top of a kiln to let out heat and aid in cooling, or to let steam escape during the early stages of firing.

Blowing: the bursting of ware caused by too-rapid rise of temperature in the kiln.

Blunger: a machine with large revolving paddles normally used to mix clay slip or glazes.

Body or clay body: a mixture of two or more clays and other earthy materials designed to meet a specific ceramic purpose.

Body stain: a specially prepared mixture of coloring oxides used to color clay.

Bone china: a dense, translucent chinaware containing considerable amounts of bone ash. It matures at about cone 6 and is not very plastic. It is produced mainly in Great Britain.

Burnishing: the act of rubbing leather-hard clay with the smooth surface of a wooden tool, a pebble, or metal tool, which gives the clay a highly polished surface. Burnishing also aids in mending cracked or broken greenware.

Calcine: heating a material in order to remove the chemically combined water. Clay is often calcined mainly to reduce excessive shrinkage.

Casting (slip casting): A method of reproducing clay forms by pouring clay slip into a hollow plaster mold, allowing it to remain long enough to thicken on the mold wall. The excess slip is poured off, and when the clay form is hard enough, it is removed.

Celadon: a pale green glaze produced by the addition of iron to the base glaze and fired in reduction.

China clay: a white firing, quite refractory, but not very plastic clay. Also known as kaolin, primary or residual clay.

Clay: any fine-grained, earthy material formed by the decomposition of feldspar, containing certain amounts of silica, alumina, water, and other minerals and, when wet, is plastic enough to be formed; when fired in red-hot heat becomes dense, glasslike, and durable.

Cones: slender, pyramid forms made of clay and specific fluxes which bend and melt at a given temperature. The cone, or pyrometric cone, measures the heat of the clay body and glaze during the firing of a kiln.

Crackle: small, hair-line cracks in the surface of a glaze.

Crawling: a glaze flaw where the glaze is pulled together leaving a separated glaze surface and caused by too heavy glaze application or uneven contraction rates between the clay body and the glaze.

Crazing: the same as crackle except that it is a glaze flaw and an undesirable effect.

Cupric and cuprous oxides: copper oxides that give mainly green colors. Under reduction firing, they may give reds.

Damp box: any area or container that maintains high humidity used to store unfinished clay objects and prevent too rapid drying of greenware.

Damper: a slab of refractory clay used to regulate the draught in kilns. It is normally used to close, or partially close, the kiln flue.

Decalcomania: a method of transferring pictures or designs from chemically treated paper to a clay form.

Deflocculent: a material such as soda ash or sodium silicate added to a casting slip to reduce the amount of water necessary to make it fluid, which in turn reduces shrinkage in drying.

Dunting: the crackling of fired clay caused by too rapid cooling of the kiln.

Earthenware: normally, a low-fired ware (usually under 2000° F.) which has an absorbency of 5 to 20 per cent.

Effervesce: to boil up, give off gas, as in the rise of bubbles in a liquid.

Engobe: a colored clay slip applied to a pot as a decoration or change of color.

Eutectic: the lowest point at which two or more materials when mixed together will melt.

Fat clay: any plastic clay, such as ball clay.

Feldspar: a mineral found in granite which contains varying amounts of alumina, silica, and either sodium, potassium, calcium, or lithium singly or in combination. It is used in clay bodies and glazes.

Ferric and ferrous oxides: iron oxides which are used mainly to give earthy brown and tan colors to clay bodies and glazes. Iron also influences the melting point of clay bodies.

1

1., 2. The slab pot takes such attitudes as the formal, calculated shape of the stoneware vase with raised clay pattern by Lyle N. Perkins (above), or the informal, free-formed shape, "Bone, Number 5," by John Stephenson (opposite).

Filler: any material that is non-plastic, such as sand, flint, or grog, used in clay bodies to control shrinkage.

Filter Press: a machine that squeezes water out of clay slip to make it into workable, semi-moist clay.

Fire: to heat in a kiln.

Fire Box: a combustion chamber for burning wood, coal, gas, or oil below the kiln.

Fireclay: any clay that is refractory, used in the manufacture of bricks and other refractory materials. It can be quite plastic and often is added to clay bodies to improve resistance to thermal shock.

Fit: the relationship of a glaze shrinkage to the clay body shrinkage. If the glaze and clay body adjust in shrinkage there is a good fit.

Flint: a form of quartz, sand, or silica found in all clays and glazes as the only glass-forming material. Silica is the only indispensable ingredient in ceramics.

Flux: any substance which causes or promotes melting.

Foot: the base of a piece of ceramics. On wheel-thrown pots, usually a trimmed, circular rim at the base.

Frit: a material which contains glass that has been melted, cooled, and then ground into a powder for use in glazes, normally to render the material insoluble.

Fuse: to melt together under heat.

Glassification: the melting of silica together with other earthy materials into a glass; turning to glass.

Glaze: a glass coating developed on clay under heat.

Greenware: any clay form that has not been fired.

Grog: clay that has been fired, then broken into small particles, normally sorted into fine, medium, or coarse sizes and added to clay bodies to reduce shrinkage, warping, and drying or firing cracks.

Ilmenite: a type of black sand containing tin and iron which, when used in granular form, produces dark specks in glazes. A quantity of about 2 to 3 per cent produces good effects.

Impermeable: in ceramics, a term that describes clay that has become nonporous or glasslike by vitrification.

Insulating brick: bricks that are extremely porous, used to reduce the loss of heat in kilns.

Kaolin: the same as China clay.

Kiln: (pronounced "kill") Any chamber, furnace, or oven used to fire clay, able to withstand very high temperatures, usually a minimum of 2000° F.

Kiln furniture: any refractory object, used inside the kiln to support ceramic ware during the firing process.

Kiln wash: a protective coating which keeps excess or runny glaze from sticking to kiln shelves and floor. Before all glaze firings, kiln shelves and floor should be painted with a coating of kiln wash. Equal parts of china clay and flint mixed with water make a good kiln wash.

Kneading: wedging or working clay like dough with the fingers or heel of the hand in order to obtain a uniform mixture.

Lead: a very common low-fired flux, best used in white lead form.

Leatherhard: partially dried clay which is firm and takes decoration well. It is the phase of drying that takes place just before the clay becomes bone dry.

Luster: a type of metallic decoration probably discovered in Egypt. A special mixture of ingredients containing a metallic salt is applied over a glaze and refired at a lower temperature which leaves a thin layer of metal on the pot.

Luting: joining leatherhard clay with slip.

Mat glaze: a dull-surfaced glaze. A mat glaze is always opaque.

Maturity: the point at which a clay body becomes vitreous or a glaze reaches the point of complete fusion.

Mold: any form used to reproduce ceramic objects. Types of molds include casting molds, press molds, hump molds, or waste molds.

Muffle: a refractory clay wall which protects ware in a kiln from direct flame.

Neutral atmosphere: an atmosphere within a kiln which is neither oxidizing nor reducing. The atmosphere in an electric kiln is considered neutral.

Non-plastic: the state of having no plasticity, not able to be shaped without cracking and breaking. Sand, grog, feldspar, and flint are some nonplastic materials.

Oil spots: lustrous metallic markings on a glaze.

Opacifier: any material that causes a transparent glaze to become opaque, the condition through which light will not pass. Tin oxide, zirconium, and titanium are excellent opacifiers.

Open: the state of clay being porous in structure.

Open firing: firing in which the flame is not baffled from the ware.

2

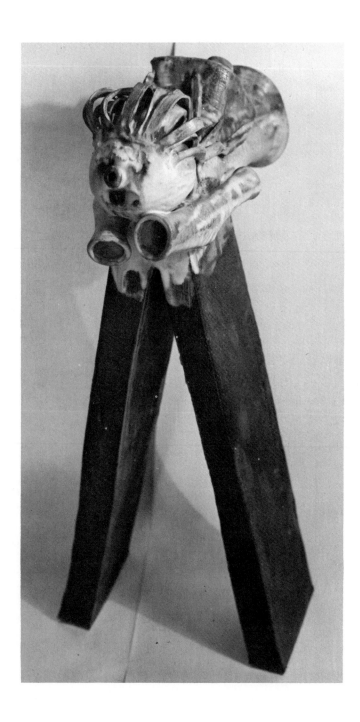

Straight forward slabs and free flowing wheel-thrown shapes are combined in this pot by the author.

Overglaze: a decoration applied over a glaze, such as the application of coloring stains.

Oxidation firing: a type of firing that allows the flame to burn completely without developing residue such as smoke, soot, or ash.

Oxide: any element combined with oxygen.

Peeling: when the clay slip or glaze separates from the surface of a pot. Peeling is caused when slip is applied when the clay body is too dry, or when the glaze is applied to a dusty surface or applied too thickly.

Peep hole: a small observation hole in the door or wall of a kiln used to watch the firing process and pyrometric cones.

Pins: small, refractory, triangular supports for ware in the kiln.

Plaster of Paris: hydrate of calcium sulphate, made by calcining gypsum. When mixed with water, it hardens and remains absorbent. It is used to dry out wet clay, to make bats and molds.

Plasticity: the ability of a material, clay, to take and hold any shape given to it.

Plastilene: clay mixed with oil in order to prevent drying. It is used in modeling forms from which molds may be cast. It is not meant to be fired.

Porcelain: a hard, non-absorbent clay body which fires white and translucent when thin. It is fired to high temperatures (normally cone 11 to 16).

Pottery: a loosely applied term, often meaning earthenware pots. Also a place where ceramic ware is produced.

Pressing: forming plastic clay against or into a mold in order to obtain a certain form.

Pug mill: a machine for mixing clay.

Pyrometer: an instrument sensitive to heat which is used to measure the temperature of the atmosphere within a kiln.

Pyrometric cones: see cones.

Quartz: a form of flint, sand or silica.

Raku: a soft, lead-glazed, groggy, freely constructed earthenware developed by the Japanese for tea ceremonies.

Raw glaze: a glaze made of insoluble ingredients which does not employ a frit. A glaze is often referred to as raw when it has been applied to a pot, but not fired.

Reducing agent: any material added to a clay body or glaze, such as silicon carbide, which combines with oxygen to form carbon monoxide during the firing process.

Reduction: a type of firing where there is incomplete burning, and smoke and soot (the excess carbon) robs the clay body and glazes of part of their oxygen, thus changing their color and texture.

Refractory: having resistance to thermal shock, melting or fusion.

Rib: a potter's tool made of metal, wood, or other material, used to shape pots, usually while working on the potter's wheel.

Saggars: a container made of refractory clay used inside kilns which do not have muffles.

Salt glaze: a glaze developed by throwing salt through a peephole into a red-hot kiln.

Sand: a form of silica, quartz, or flint.

Secondary clay: any clay that has been formed by being transported by wind, water, or glacier from the site of its parent rock. Also called sedimentary clay.

Sgraffito: a method of decorating ware by scratching through a colored clay slip to show the contrasting body color underneath.

Shard: a broken piece of ceramics, sometimes called a sherd.

Short: the property of slight plasticity in a clay body.

Silt: loose sedimentary material suspended in water.

Single fire: a one-step firing process in which a piece of ceramics is fired to maturity without a bisque firing.

Slip: normally, a mixture of clay suspended in water to the consistency of heavy cream.

Slurry: another term for clay slip; slip that is uneven in consistency.

Spraying: a method of applying a glaze with a compressed-air spray gun.

Sprigging: applying plastic coils or wads of clay to a pot to form a relief decoration.

Stack: placing ware inside a kiln.

Stain: either a single coloring oxide or a combination of oxides used as an overglaze, to color clay bodies, or as glaze colorants.

Stilts: any refractory clay piece used to support ceramic ware. Also called spurs, pins, and posts.

Stoneware: ceramics fired to a temperature between 2150°F. and 2350°F. A body that has very little absorption

and which is completely opaque; extremely hard and dense.

Terra cotta: a common sculpture clay body with lots of grog and usually red in color; an earthenware body.

Terra sigillatta: a very fine grained slip glaze which, when applied, is burnished and fired to give a glaze-like surface. Produced originally during the Etruscan and Greek periods of ancient history.

Throwing: making ceramics on the potter's wheel.

Trailing: a decoration method in which clay slip is applied to leather-hard pot from a rubber syringe.

Translucent: the stage of being able to admit light, but not being transparent.

Transparent: capable of being seen through, as in window glass; or, in ceramics, a clear glaze.

Turning: trimming the foot of a ceramic form on the potter's wheel while the clay is leatherhard.

Underglaze: any colored decoration applied on bisque ware before the glaze is applied.

Viscosity: the property of resisting flow, stiffness.

Vitreous: glass-like. The state of a clay body or glaze when it has been fired to maturity.

Volatilization: the action produced within a firing kiln where some materials are changed from a solid to a gaseous state, such as water turning to steam.

Wad: any small piece of plastic clay which is normally used to level shelves when stacking a kiln.

Ware: any kind of pottery, ceramics in any form; raw, bisque, or glazed.

Water glass: sodium silicate.

Water smoking: the first stage of the firing cycle up to a dull red heat, 1000° to 1100° F., which allows for atmospheric and chemically combined water to escape.

Wax resist: a way of decorating a clay form by applying a design with a liquid wax solution or emulsion and applying a coat of stain, clay slip, or glaze over. The wax prevents the stain, slip, or glaze from adhering to the pot, thereby producing a contrasting color or texture on the ware.

Weathering: exposing clay to wind, rain, and outside atmosphere, which renders the clay more plastic.

Wedging: a method to make clay homogeneous. Another name for kneading.

Wicket: the door of a kiln.

Win: to mine or dig clay.

1

GLAZE RECIPES

The development of a specific glaze can be just as rewarding as any other phase of the ceramic process. Until recently, many potters kept their glaze formulas secret. Now, glaze recipes can easily be obtained from published literature. The following is a brief list of some glaze recipes:

(1)
Cone 08, Lead glaze. A good clear glaze when applied thinly.
White lead 55.0
Feldspar 21.5
Flint 16.8
Whiting 4.5
Zinc oxide 1.2
Clay 9

(2)
Cone 08 - 06, Lead glaze. An excellent glaze for raku firing.
White lead 70.0
Flint 26.0
Kaolin 4.0

(3)
Cone 04 - 03, Mat glaze. Avoid thick application.
Clinchfield feldspar 48.0
Whiting 13.5
Barium carbonate 13.5
Colemanite 11.0
Flint 10.0
Zinc oxide 4.0

(4)
Cone 9 - 10, Mat glaze. Good results can be obtained in reduction or oxidation firing.
Clinchfield feldspar 52.4
Barium carbonate 20.6
Yankee ball clay 10.1
Whiting 9.5
Zinc oxide 7.4

Symbols for common ceramic oxides and elements.

Aluminum Oxide	Al_2O_3
Aluminum	Al
Antimony Oxide	Sb_2O_3
Antimony	Sb
Barium Oxide	BaO
Barium	Ba
Boric Oxide	B_2O_3
Boron	B
Calcium Oxide	CaO
Calcium	Ca
Carbon	C
Chromium Oxide	Cr_2O_3
Chromium	Cr
Cobalt Oxide	Co_2O_3
Cobalt	Co
Copper Oxide	CuO
Copper	Cu
Iron Oxide	Fe_2O_3
Iron	Fe
Lead Oxide	PbO
Lead	Pb
Lithium Oxide	Li_2O
Lithium	Li
Magnesium Oxide	MgO
Magnesium	Mg
Manganese Dioxide	MnO_2
Manganese	Mn
Nickel Oxide	NiO
Nickel	Ni
Potassium Oxide	K_2O
Potassium	K
Silicon Dioxide	SiO_2
Silicon	Si
Sodium Oxide	Na_2O
Sodium	Na
Strontium Oxide	SrO
Strontium	Sr

Tin Oxide	SnO
Tin	Sn
Titanium	Ti
Vanadium	V
Zinc Oxide	ZnO
Zinc	Zn
Zirconium Oxide	ZrO_2
Zirconium	Zr

Converting Centigrade to Fahrenheit and Fahrenheit to Centigrade

To convert Centigrade to Fahrenheit, use the following formula:

$$F = \frac{Centigrade}{5} \times 9 + 32$$

Example: Cone 9 = 1285 Centigrade. What degree Fahrenheit is cone 9?

$$\frac{1285°}{5} \times 9 + 32 = F \qquad F = 2345°$$

To convert Fahrenheit to Centigrade, use the following formula:

$$C = \frac{Fahrenheit - 32}{9} \times 5$$

Example: Cone 06 = 1859° Fahrenheit. What degree Centigrade is cone 06?

$$\frac{1859 - 32}{9} \times 5 = C \qquad C = 1015$$

Water of plasticity of clay

The more water required to make dry powdered clay plastic and workable the more it will shrink as it dries. Any clay dug from a new site should be tested for water of plasticity so that it may be altered, if necessary, to meet the potter's needs. A very simple test is to grind up a dry sample of the clay into powder form. Next, carefully

1. The textural quality of a plate or bowl should be smooth on the interior surface if it is to serve its normal function of holding food or water. However, as a decorative piece, the texture may be an important part of the work as seen in this plate. Ljerka Javan Saric, Yugoslavia.

2. Utilizing the thrown form gives the necessary strength to construct this black stoneware, 36 inch high, "Dancing Woman." Raul Angulo Coronel, U.S.A.

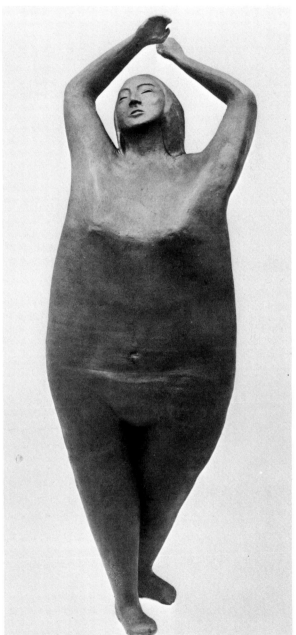

2

weigh out 500 grams of clay. Pour 500 cc. of water into a graduated beaker. With the clay on a glass plate, pour slowly a little water at a time to the clay. Keep mixing the clay until it is the desired consistency for working. Be careful not to add too much water. Determine the amount of water necessary to make the clay plastic. The following formula will give the water of plasticity:

$$\text{Percent of water of plasticity} = \frac{\text{Weight of water}}{\text{Weight of dry clay}} \times 100$$

Tests for shrinkage
Knowing how much a clay body will shrink is important to the potter. Clay shrinks in its greenware state as well as during the firing process.

Drying shrinkage of greenware
Wedge up a ball of clay of normal working consistency and roll out slabs about 6 inches long, one inch wide, and ¼ inch thick. Mark on the slab with a pointed tool a line exactly 4 inches long. Allow the slabs to become bone dry, turning them frequently so that they will not warp. Then, measure the length of the line. The percent of shrinkage can be calculated by the following formula:

$$\text{Percent of shrinkage} = \frac{\text{plastic length of line} - \text{dry length of line}}{\text{plastic length of line}} \times 100$$

Shrinkage of fired ware
This test should be done at different temperatures to find the rate of shrinkage. The dried slabs of clay used in the previous test should be fired. The length of the line is measured on the dried bar and then on the fired bar. The amount of shrinkage is calculated as follows:

$$\text{Percent of shrinkage} = \frac{\text{dry length of line} - \text{fired length of line}}{\text{dry length of line}} \times 100$$

The entire shrinkage from plastic clay to fired clay can also be calculated.

$$\text{Percent of shrinkage} = \frac{\text{plastic length of clay} - \text{fired length of clay}}{\text{plastic length of clay}} \times 100$$

Water absorption of fired clay
Depending upon the temperature that clay is fired, it will be more or less vitreous, and will absorb water at comparative rates. The more vitreous the clay after it has been fired, the less water it will absorb. In order to know just how mature a clay body is when it is fired at a specific temperature, a simple test may be conducted.

Make a few slabs of clay, just as in shrinkage tests, and fire each one at separate temperatures. The fired pieces are then carefully weighed. Then the fired slabs of clay are boiled in water for at least two hours. They are then removed from the water, and the excess water is patted off the surface. The pieces are weighed again. The following formula is used to calculate the amount of water absorption:

$$\text{Absorption percentage} = \frac{\text{Wet weight of clay} - \text{dry weight of clay}}{\text{Dry weight of clay}} \times 100$$

1

1. Thrown stoneware spherical form with a glaze pattern, 12 inches high. Minnie Negoro, U.S.A.

2. The potter has achieved a very interesting effect by combining a sheet copper base to this slab-built form; 30 inches tall, reduced stoneware. Llye N. Perkins, U.S.A.

REFERENCES

Books

Ball, F. Carlton and Lovoos, Janice, *Making Pottery Without a Wheel.* New York: Reinhold, 1965.

Kenny, John B., *The Complete Book of Pottery Making.* Philadelphia: Chilton, 1949.

Leach, Bernard, *A Potter's Book.* Transatlantic Arts, 1951.

Nelson, Glenn C., *Ceramics, A Potter's Handbook.* New York: Holt, Rinehart and Winston, 1960.

Rhodes, Daniel, *Clay and Glazes for the Potter.* Philadelphia: Chilton, 1957.

———, *Stoneware and Porcelain.* Philadelphia: Chilton, 1959.

Magazines

Ceramics Monthly, 4175 N. High St., Columbus, Ohio 43201.

Craft Horizons, 29 West 53rd St., New York, N.Y. 10019.

Design Quarterly, Walker Art Center, 1710 Lyndale Ave. S., Minneapolis, Minnesota 55403.

School Arts, Davis Publications, Inc., 50 Portland St., Worcester, Mass. 01608.

2

TEMPERATURE EQUIVALENTS FOR STANDARD PYROMETRIC CONES

As determined at the National Bureau of Standards

Large cones	cone number	^{1}60°C	108°F	150°C	270°F
	022	585°C.	1085°F.	600°C.	1112°F.
	021	602	1116	614	1137
	020	625	1157	635	1175
	019	668	1234	683	1261
	018	696	1285	717	1323
	017	727	1341	747	1377
	016	764	1407	792	1458
	015	790	1454	804	1479
	014	834	1533	838	1540
	013	869	1596	852	1566
	012	866	1591	884	1623
	011	886	1627	894	1641
	†010	887	1629	894	1641
	09	915	1679	923	1693
	08	945	1733	955	1751
	07	973	1783	984	1803
	06	991	1816	999	1830
	05	1031	1888	1046	1915
	04	1050	1922	1060	1940
	03	1086	1987	1101	2014
	02	1101	2014	1120	2048
	01	1117	2043	1137	2079
	1	1136	2077	1154	2109
	2	1142	2088	1162	2124
	3	1152	2106	1168	2134
	4	1168	2134	1186	2167
	5	1177	2151	1196	2185
	6	1201	2194	1222	2232
	7	1215	2219	1240	2264
	8	1236	2257	1263	2305
	9	1260	2300	1280	2336
	10	1285	2345	1305	2381
	11	1294	2361	1315	2399
	12	1306	2383	1326	2419
	13	1321	2410	1346	2455
	14	1388	2530	1366	2491
	15	1424	2595	1431	2608

Small cones	cone number	300°C	540°F	
	022	630°C.*	1165°F.*	* Temperatures approximate. See Note 3.
	021	643	1189	
	020	666	1231	† Iron-free (white) are made in numbers 010 to 3. The iron-free cones have the same deformation temperatures as the equivalents shown in italics when fired at a rate of 60 Centigrade degrees per hour in air.
	019	723	1333	
	018	752	1386	
	017	784	1443	
	016	825	1517	
	015	843	1549	*Notes:*
	014	870*	1596	1. The temperature equivalents in this table apply only to Orton Standard Pyrometric Cones, *when heated at the rates indicated, in an air atmosphere.*
	013	880*	1615	
	012	900*	1650	
	011	915*	1680	2. Temperature Equivalents are given in degrees Centigrade (°C.) and the corresponding degrees Fahrenheit
	†010	919	1686	(°F.). The rates of heating shown at the head of each column of temperature equivalents were maintained during the last several hundred degrees of temperature rise.
	09	955	1751	
	08	983	1801	
	07	1008	1846	
	06	1023	1873	
	05	1062	1944	3. The temperature equivalents were determined at the National Bureau of Standards by H.P. Beerman (See Journal of the American Ceramic Society, Vol. 39, 1956), with the exception of those marked (*).
	04	1098	2008	
	03	1131	2068	
	02	1148	2098	
	01	1178	2152	
	1	1179	2154	4. The temperature equivalents are not necessarily those at which cones will deform under firing conditions different from those under which the calibrating determinations were made. For more detailed technical data, please write the Orton Foundation.
	2	1179	2154	
	3	1196	2185	
	4	1209	2208	
	5	1221	2230	
	6	1255	2291	5. For reproducible results, care should be taken to insure that the cones are set in a plaque with the bending face at the correct angle of 8° from the vertical, with the cone tips at the correct height above the top of the plaque. (Large Cone 2", small cones 15/16")
	7	1264	2307	
	8	1300	2372	
	9	1317	2403	
	10	1330	2426	
	11	1336	2437	
	12	1355	2471	

The Edward Orton Jr. Ceramic Foundation.